MW00617396

Bean There, Donor That

A Journey of Random Donation

by Rick Daynes

copyright 2024 Rick Daynes
rickdaynes@gmail.com
Published by: Showme Publishing,
14520 Camino de la Luna No. 2
San Diego, CA 92127
Cover Art: Bryan Niven
Graphic Work: Shaun Miner
Editing: Jennifer Gadbow

Dedication

To the thousands of people waiting for a healthy organ, eye, or tissue. Also, to the donors who save lives. To my sister-in-law, Lindsey. All you did was open your mouth. It was a simple act, yet it connected two families who will never be the same.

Introduction

Every now and then I get on a journal kick. I wish I was on it consistently, but that has never been the case. Luckily, I was on it when my kidney adventure began, and I continued until well after the organ was harvested. This book chronicles that experience. It is a journey of the adventure from beginning to end.

Most of my journal was transcribed from voice recordings on my cell phone. During dramatic moments, I would steal away and record in real time what was going on. It was therapeutic and fun, and it helped me navigate the process and understand it better.

I omitted most, but not all of my slang and verbal expressions that did not translate well to the page. I cannot believe I said, "I was like…she was like…we were like…" so much. My nerdy research of the human body and science behind this process was also trimmed to keep you engaged. At least, that is my hope. I circle a lot of subjects and I've included a few surprises. There certainly were plenty of those for me. Lastly, you will see from the chapter titles that music is always running through my brain. I had fun with this part; feel free to sing along.

I decided to tell this story because I wanted to do more to further the cause of organ, tissue, and eye donation. I wrote it for my family and for myself, and I am publishing it six years after I became single. That is to say, I only have one kidney now and not two. Nowhere do I suggest that living donation is for everyone or y'all better register those kidneys today.

No, it's not for everyone, but it was for me. Maybe someday, it might be for you too.

At the conclusion of this journal, I think you will not only have a better sense of why someone would donate an organ, but why, at least for me, it became so important that I fought for it. It was never one of my life goals. It wasn't even on my radar. Yet it became a defining moment for me. In retrospect, this short journey was a microcosm of my life. Battles were won and lost, emotions ran the gauntlet, and we forged ahead to become better people.

Enjoy.

Bean There, Donor That

A Journey of Random Donation

PART 1

QUEST

June 25, 2017 (Tropic, Utah)

We Are Family - Sister Sledge

Hanging Day at Daynes Family Reunions (DFRs) is always righteous. We never planned any big activities on that day. Playing games on the lawn, lounging around, catching up and reconnecting with family–that's what it was all about. Today, my sister-in-law, Lindsey, and I were in the family room, talking about this and that. She asked if I remembered someone named Jenny Petersen. I said, "nope." Lindsey told me that I had indeed met Jenny when Lindsey and my brother, Ozz, brought eight families with them from Farmington, Utah to camp at San Elijo State Beach for the week. She said that Jenny had a child with Down Syndrome. When she said that, a light went off. I did remember. Our son, Eli, also has Down Syndrome. He was a mere eight weeks old that year and I remembered that we were looking forward to meeting Jenny's son.

Lindsey then told me that Jenny needed a kidney transplant. She said that Jenny had already lost one kidney and that her remaining kidney was failing. Her doctors had told the family to start compiling a list of donors because they had not found a match among any of their family members or friends. I looked at Lindsey and I heard these words come out of my mouth: "Shoot, put me on the list."

June 26, 2017

On The Road Again - Willie Nelson

Today my wife, Robin, my kids, and I were driving home from Utah. The ride is not short and it ain't easy. Tonight, we would stay in Las Vegas; tomorrow, we would be home.

I had started to feel like donating my kidney to Jenny might be something I was destined to do, and I wanted to talk to Robin about it. I said, "You know how things just kinda happen to me? Well, sometimes I feel like Forrest Gump. He got to witness and participate in all of these fascinating and historical things and he was there at exactly the right time. Well, it's like that with Jenny–I feel like this is something maybe I was meant to do."

We talked about the Petersen family and what they must be going through. It was hard for either of us to put ourselves in their shoes. Jenny was a young mother with four kids. Her oldest son had just turned 15 and had Down Syndrome. Robin and I both agreed that Jenny was someone who had a lot of people counting on her and who had a lot to live for. Robin then decided she would be tested too, to see if she was a match for the transplant.

Something popped into my head that I hadn't thought about before: Would my O negative blood type make me a likely match? I knew that my blood type made me a universal blood donor, but I did not know how this would impact my suitability as a kidney donor. I asked my nurse wife about it, and she said "yes, absolutely," and explained why.

As she spoke, my kids' ears perked up. There is a touch of nerd in those kids, and mom was talking science. Robin explained that people with O negative blood type are considered universal donors because they can donate to people with any blood type. This is because O negative blood lacks A, B, and Rh factors that could cause immune reactions in the recipient. Therefore, O negative donors are generally compatible with a broader range of recipients.

I already knew the universal donor part and that I was RH negative. I was also CMV negative, but I didn't know what that meant so I asked Robin. She said that CMV is a chronic infection that is spread by close contact with someone who has CMV in their saliva, urine, or other body fluids. It stays in the body for life. In the United States, the CMV infection rate is estimated to be between 50% and 80%. In healthy people, it often causes no symptoms, and you can live your entire life without knowing you have it. However, CMV is one of the most dangerous infections for transplant patients and can cause major problems. The fact that I was CMV negative was a score.

With all of this talk about O negative, RH, and CMV, of course I had to tell my baby donor story and how I was Captain Baby Donor.

Captain Baby Donor

I told the kids that my mom and dad are both O negative blood types and they produced a whole family of O negative kids, of which I am one. Then I told them, when we lived in Key West, the bloodmobile would park outside my office every six weeks. Someone in the bloodmobile would either call or enter our building and ask the receptionist to ring my office. When I walked out of my office, everyone would ask why they were calling me. At the time, I thought it was because they knew I would come. I wasn't thinking too much about my blood type.

When we moved to San Diego, I continued to donate blood. I gave to the local blood bank and the Red Cross. I got calls and emails all the time telling me they were in desperate need of my blood type. I just figured they said that to everyone. So I decided to find out. I said to the woman who called me, "I know you tell everyone that." She told me that my blood was the most sought after because I was a universal donor. My mother had told me this my entire adult life but I didn't really think about what it meant. She'd say, "You kids should give blood as much as possible because God blessed you with a gift you could share with everyone in need."

Although I already knew I was a universal donor, I never really thought about the other types of blood being in short supply or what happened to my blood after I gave or who I might be helping. You lie down, give blood, get your cookie, and walk away.

One day, I noticed a bloodmobile outside the Souplantation restaurant. They were giving away a free meal at the Soupy for giving blood. Well I was all over that! Only problem was I did not have time to stand in that long line. So I thought I would see how much they really needed my blood. I went to the sign-up desk and said, "I'm sorry, I have an appointment at work and cannot wait in this line. But I am O negative and I would like to give."

The woman punched my name into the database and all my information came up. She excused herself and walked into the bloodmobile. Twenty seconds later, she returned with someone in scrubs who handed me a fist full of cookies and an apple juice. The woman in scrubs thanked me for coming and took me directly onto the bus. She then asked if I would give double the red blood cells?

She explained that they had a machine that pumped my blood out and separated the red blood cells. Then it returned the plasma and platelets along with some saline, and then drew another batch. I then selfishly asked, "If I am giving double the red blood cells, can I get double the prize so I can take my wife to dinner?" She walked away and returned with two coupons for the Soupy. I'm in!

While giving blood, the woman attending me said, "You're a baby donor." I had never heard that term before and assumed she was talking about my blood type. She said, "Most people are CMV positive. Most people are also RH positive. You are O negative, so you can give to anyone. But you are also CMV negative and that makes you a baby donor. You are also RH negative, so you have pretty much the best blood we could ask for."

Well look who is feeling special now! Armed with this new information and two coupons to Souplantation, I set off on my quest for free stuff for giving blood. I scored two more dinner freebies for another date night with the wife, took the kids to a mini amusement park, and even got ski lift vouchers!

I had officially become a blood donor snob. When I arrived at the bloodmobile, they rolled out the red carpet. I'd say, "Hey, I'm gonna help myself to some granola bars and OJ before I pump out a pint, cool?" I started using that new language, O negative, RH negative, CMV negative. I was not waiting in any lines and I was scoring double the prizes for double the red blood cells. I was a baby donor, after all!

I'll admit, I got away from the real reason I should be donating. I needed a good shot in the arm. And I got it too. I started thinking about what it meant to be a baby donor. Plus, I had been stuck so many times, a good amount of scar tissue had developed and it was becoming harder to stick my veins. Twice, someone had to move the needle around while it was in my arm to get the vein, and that was no fun. So, my donations and my baby donor ego cooled down.

June 28, 2017 (San Diego)

Start Me Up - The Rolling Stones

Got home from DFR late last night. This morning, I was greeted by a mountain of emails, including one from Lindsey that she sent while I was on my way home. It was from Steve Petersen, Jenny's husband. It read:

June 10, 2017

Dear Family and Friends,

Two years ago, Jenny found out she had likely been born with only one functioning kidney. While the doctors assured us everything would be fine and not to worry, that kidney has steadily declined. My wife is now in end-stage kidney failure and has been referred to the transplant team at the University of Utah. She will be listed on the national registry to be a kidney recipient within the next few days.

Soon, to stay alive, Jenny will need either a kidney transplant or to go on dialysis. While dialysis is a temporary option, we desperately want to avoid going that route. Dialysis, even as a bridge to a kidney transplant, has serious negative side effects that would adversely impact Jenny's health while she is receiving treatment and would dramatically shorten the life of a donated kidney.

Through the national registry, Jenny is eligible to receive a deceased-donor kidney. Nationally, the median time to receive a deceased-donor transplant is seven years. At the University of Utah Health, the average is about three years. There are currently 100,000+ people on the national waiting list. Waiting for a deceased-donor kidney would almost certainly mean long-term dialysis treatment for Jenny.

Jenny's best path to receiving a kidney is through a living donor. Asking someone to consider donating a kidney is extremely difficult and humbling. However, this selfless act would provide my wife with her greatest chance of an extended life. A kidney from a living donor generally lasts twice as long as a deceased-donor kidney and has better function. I would encourage you to become informed about living donation at:

www.kidney.org/transplantation/livingdonors

Here are a few basic yet important facts:

• A donor only needs one kidney to live a healthy, long life, and longevity of the donor is rarely affected.

• Most donor surgery is done laparoscopically (tiny incisions).

• The recuperation period is fairly quick…generally a two- to three-day hospital stay and two to three weeks of rest.

- The cost of being evaluated and, ultimately, the cost of surgery for the donor would be covered by my insurance.

- You would have a separate team of healthcare professionals to evaluate you as a living donor. Their job is to help you understand the risks of transplant and to look out for your best interests.

If you would be willing to consider donating a kidney to Jenny, please follow these steps.

1. Navigate to www.uofulivingdonor.org.
2. Choose to be evaluated as a Living Kidney Donor.
3. Complete the online health history questionnaire.
4. Under "Donor Type" choose Named Recipient, and input Jenny Petersen.

When we met with the transplant team earlier this week, we were encouraged to invite any and all to serve as a kidney donor and not to disqualify anyone based on known medical conditions. They encouraged us to get as many people as we possibly could to come forward in the next seven days to give them a pool to work with. The transplant team will determine the order in which potential live donors are tested. Please know that we understand the weight of this decision, and signing up now does not mean you can't ultimately decide not to donate at a later time.

Although the timing of the transplant surgery remains unknown, Jenny's kidney has declined to a point that the time for getting things in order is now. The actual transplant surgery could still be months away. Neither Jenny nor I will be following up with you on this email.

We know that the decision to donate an organ is a personal one, and that many individual factors come into play when making such a decision. Please know the online health history questionnaire is private...we will not know who has signed up and who has not. We appreciate your careful consideration of this donation. Please feel free to forward this letter to any you think may be interested.

Independent of your decision, we greatly appreciate your friendship and support. We have been surrounded by so much love as we have faced this trial. I ask for your continued prayers and support of Jenny as we navigate this process...it is more meaningful and impactful than you know.

Sincerely,

Steve Petersen

I read the email to Robin. We both felt a tremendous amount of compassion. How could we not? I asked Robin if she felt good about me signing up. She said, "Of course! What if that was me, Rick? What if I needed a kidney? Wouldn't you want someone to step up and help us?" I said, "Okay, here it goes..." I clicked on the link, filled out the questions, and put myself on the list. Robin asked me to sign her up as well, but I told her I did not feel good about that. We have five kids including a four-year-old with Down Syndrome. They, and especially Eli, need Robin to be around for a long time. I would rather not compromise Robin's health in any way, as Eli needs her more than he needs me.

July 3, 2017

Another Brick in the Wall - Pink Floyd

Got a letter from the University of Utah Medical Center today. Basically, says thanks for signing up and states they are working on the list of possible donors. It's hard to imagine they could not find a donor within Jenny or Steve's family or circle of friends. I mean, they both come from big families, and big families have a lot of friends, including my brother who lives close to them. I'm glad I signed up (you only need one kidney, right?) but I'll never get called. I'm sure there are a ton of people on the list.

August 18, 2017

Another One Bites the Dust - Queen

Talked to my brother Ozz on the phone today. As our conversation was winding down, I thought about Jenny. I figured they had gone through a couple hundred possible donors by now and most likely had a match. Ozz told me about the movement in their community and beyond to find a donor. He said lots of people were being tested. He told me that he had a feeling he was a match and that he was the one who would be donating. He said it was really frustrating to wait for the clinic to call him with the results and then disappointing to find out he was not a match.

Since I am 800 miles away and out of state, I figured that I was at the bottom of the barrel. And since my

11

brother wasn't a match, they probably removed my name from the list.

October 24, 2017

Call Me Maybe - Carley Rae Jepsen

Got a call today from an 801-area code. Ninety-eight percent of the time, when I don't know who is calling, I let it go to voicemail. For some reason, this time, I picked it up. Some woman on the other end said she was a nurse from the University of Utah Transplant Department. Because I was only half-way listening, I told her she must have the wrong number. She then told me I was on the list to be tested for Jenny Petersen's kidney transplant. I asked her to repeat herself. And then I asked again. Midway through her third attempt, I realized what she was talking about!

"Yes! Yes! Yes! I'm sorry, I did not realize this was still going on. I was under the impression, just cause it's been a while and I know the list was big, that a donor had been found." She told me they were still looking, and asked if I was willing to be tested. I told her I would be tested, but that they were likely wasting their time with me. I explained that my brother, who was friends with the Petersens, had already been tested and was not a match.

She said they would still like to test me. I said, "You sure? We have the same parents, same blood type, same flimsy ears, same booty, and same alien-like keel on the top of our heads. How could he not be a match and I would be?" I continued, "And frankly, how could all those family members and friends who have

12

been tested not be compatible?" Then she explained something that blew me away.

She said that sometimes a transplant recipient has antibodies in their blood that react against the kidney and damage and/or reject it. These antibodies might develop due to the environment, pregnancy, genetics, personal health history, and/or previous exposure. People living near each other, like the relatives and friends that were being tested for Jenny's transplant, might have been exposed to similar environmental factors, including pathogens like bacteria and viruses. As a result, they might have developed similar antibodies against common infectious agents.

She continued to explain that before an organ transplant, a laboratory procedure is conducted called a cross-match test, to assess the compatibility between the donor and recipient. For a kidney transplant, the cross-match test specifically involves testing for the presence of antibodies in the recipient's blood that could react with the donor's cells. A positive cross-match indicates a higher risk of kidney rejection.

"Whoa, whoa, whoa!" I exclaimed. "Just hold on there! Every kidney transplant story I have ever heard has been from a family member. A brother donating to a brother or dad or something along those lines. What you are telling me does not make sense. Jenny has four children, so I get the pregnancy antibody issue. But are you telling me that a non-relative from the other side of the world has a better chance of being a match than a relative who lives in the same area?"

The nurse responded, "Exactly. Being from far away or even of a different race suggests your antibodies will be negative, and that is what you want. Does your brother live close to the recipient?" "Yes," I replied. "He has lived in the same neighborhood for maybe ten years, which I'm guessing is enough time to absorb the same antibodies. Plus, he spent two years in the jungle in Brazil, so who knows what kind of rare tropical fungus he is carrying."

Our conversation continued:

Nurse: Ten years would certainly be enough time to absorb those antibodies.

Me: So why do I only hear about family members donating? Is it because they are family and the first or maybe the only people to volunteer?

Nurse: Yes. You know there are currently 120,000 people on the national transplant registry, waiting for a kidney? Many of them have family members or friends who have volunteered, but for whatever reason, they are not a good match.

Me: Wait, what?!!! 120,000 people?! That's unbelievable!

Nurse: Yes, and 5,000 of those people die every year waiting for a kidney.

Me: Are you serious?!!! And that's just in the United States?!!!

Nurse: Yes. And there are other factors involved, but we would still like to test you.

Me: What the heck, let's give it a go.

Nurse: After you visit the lab, you should hear back from us in a week to 10 days.

October 30, 2017

Message in a Bottle - The Police

UPS delivered a kit today from the Solid Organ Transplant Center. As I looked at the package, and focused on those words, THE SOLID ORGAN TRANSPLANT CENTER, things got real. I had spoken to Ozz earlier that day and I knew that things were getting dicey for the Petersen family. Jenny's remaining kidney was declining steadily. I figured I would get this done ASAP, so I fired off an email to my doc asking him the quickest way to go about this. I busted out the kit, scanned the instructions, and emailed them to him.

October 31, 2017

Return to Sender - Elvis Presley

Happy Halloween! Thought I'd celebrate the occasion by visiting Dracula's lair and getting some blood sucked out of my veins. I know my blood is sweet because nobody attracts mosquitoes like me! I'm like a human pin cushion. In any case, the lab experience could have been a little smoother. Because the request came from out of state, there were phone calls and approvals that needed to happen. And, of course, the someone who needed to make that happen was at lunch. I got comfortable in the waiting room until all the busy work was completed.

My lab tech, Mr. Stick, read the instructions over (and over), found a good vein, and I was out the door with a package full of vials of my blood. I still felt like I probably was not a match, just like everyone else wasn't. I took the kit to the nearest UPS store and shipped it back to the med center. Should have results in a week to 10 days.

November 1, 2017

Hot Blooded - Foreigner

Got a call today from the nurse/transplant coordinator at the med center (Teresa). They got the samples, but somehow, we screwed up on the directions because they also needed the lab to test my blood type. I was a little irritated.

Me: Shooooot! That's the easiest thing I've ever heard! I'm O negative!

Teresa: We need something official.

Me: I'm officially telling you my blood type is O negative. My mom is O negative, my dad is O negative, and they raised a family of seven boys and one girl and, guess what? All O negative.

Teresa: I'm sure you are O negative, but unless we get something in writing from an agency, we are going to need you to go back in and get retested.

Me: No problem. I have an official blood card from the Red Cross and the San Diego Blood Bank declaring the red fluid flowing through my veins is O negative. And believe me, these guys know my blood type. They call me every month asking for my blood. I will scan it and send it to you right away.

Teresa: Can we get something from your doctor's office?

Me: You won't accept an official blood card from the biggest blood suckers on the planet? Who knows blood better than THE BLOOD BANK?!

Teresa eventually accepted the blood bank card with the provision that if her bosses did not accept it, I would have to do a little leg work. Hoping I don't have to. After all, I sent them half a dozen tubes of my blood. Can't they test one of them?! I scanned my Blood Bank card and sent the following email:

Teresa,

Attached is an official document from the best blood source in the world. Please accept this Red Cross Blood Bank card as proof of my blood type so I don't have to track down a nurse to get that information to you.

Thanks,

Rick Daynes

December 7, 2017

You're the One That I Want - John Travolta & Olivia Newton-John

I got the call on Pearl Harbor Day. I had driven out to Palm Springs early that morning and the day was not going well. Normally, when I drive to the Valley, I spend the mornings with my best clients and the rest of the day visiting old customers and/or drumming up new business. Today, I was expecting some reorders and also had some new products I was sure to get into my stores. Instead, I lost an account, and my other customers didn't reorder anything. I felt physically sick. Not just because I was having a hard day with work, but... well, I couldn't really put my finger on it. And I cannot really tell you what my symptoms were. I just felt off. So, with my tail between my legs, I scooted out of the Valley and onto the freeway for the two-and-a-half-hour drive home.

I called Robin to tell her I did not feel well, and that I would be home early. While we were speaking, another call came in. Unsure of who the caller was (I was on Bluetooth and my phone was on the floor), I told Robin I would call her back and switched over.

Me: Hi, this is Rick.

Caller: Hi, this is Teresa with the University of Utah Transplant Center.

Me: I'm sorry, who is this?

Caller: This is Teresa with the Transplant Center. I would like to talk to you about your blood test.

Me: Oh Teresa! How are you? I'm sorry, it's been a while. What's going on?

Teresa: Yes, I'm sorry I didn't get back to you sooner. Things are so busy around here and...

My brain: The kidney thing was fresh on my mind five, even four weeks ago. Teresa told me they would call me with results in a week to 10 days, although my brother did tell me they took three weeks to get back to him. I knew they had exhausted all Utah volunteers and who knows where else they have been testing for this case before they got to me?

I had completely dismissed myself as a donor more than two weeks ago. If I were a match for the transplant, surely, they would have gotten back to me sooner. After three weeks I thought, because I didn't get a call, I was just like everyone before me: DENIED! In fact, I had actually started formulating a plan to help the Petersens find a donor. I don't really know them, but we both have kids with Down Syndrome. And if there is one thing I know, it's that the Down Syndrome community is strong, passionate, and full of love. I thought I would ask the Petersens if we could help by appealing to this audience, and, if we needed to, take it to the entire special needs club.

I was prepared for the denial talk and was sure this conversation would be over soon. I started thinking of my plan to help Jenny find a donor and was wondering if they would go for that. I mean, I'm basically a stranger and...then, these words:

Teresa: ...and you ARE a blood and tissue match with the recipient.

Me:
[Pause..
........................still pausing.................................
....] I'm sorry. What???!!

Teresa: You are a good match for the recipient. We need to know if you would like to proceed.

[Pause....................crickets......................................
.... brain not functioning.]

"If you would like to proceed" came over all four speakers of my car and it sounded like James Earl Jones was speaking at a penetrating volume. Time slowed as my brain tried to process what she was saying.

Teresa: Rick? Are you there?

Me: YES! NO! WAIT! NO! I MEAN YES! WAIT! Can we back up for a minute? I know this is rude, but can you repeat everything you just said? I need to understand this.

For the next twenty minutes, Teresa explained what was happening and where we would go from here. I then restated everything to make sure I understood. We talked about the blood and urine tests I would be taking, the visits to the medical center, and the time involved. We talked briefly about mental health, family, and financial considerations.

Suddenly, I felt like somebody was shaking me by the shoulders and I realized that Teresa was conducting an interview! Just being a physical match isn't good enough to give a kidney; I had to be ready for the long road ahead. Then we discussed requirements.

This was a little weird because Teresa was talking to me like this was actually going to happen. There was no, "if," you pass this. Rather, everything she said was "when" you pass this and "after" you do that. I took a deep breath and relaxed a bit. I told myself that this was standard procedure for everyone who gets to this point. Then I asked Teresa how many people in the Petersen pool had reached this point. Teresa responded in her James Earl Jones' voice, "Zero." Shocked, I asked "How many people in the pool are you still testing?" Again, James Earl Jones: "Zero."

Me: ZERO?

Teresa: YOU ARE IT.

Me: I AM IT??!!?!!!?!! WHAT!!!?

Everything slowed down again as I heard James Earl Jones tell me that there were no backups and that I. WAS. IT. I regained enough composure for James to morph back into Nurse Teresa so I could attempt to communicate somewhat coherently. I am a numbers guy. I need statistics. What I thought was a one in a million shot, had now, I was sure, significantly increased.

I asked Teresa, "What percentage of people, from where I am right now, end up actually on the operating table?" She said about 80%. Teresa kept talking, but again, her voice trailed off because all I could think about was, HOLY CRAP! In the blink of an eye, I went from one in a million to 80%! There is right now an 80% chance that I am letting someone cut into me and take an organ out of my body.

Teresa also said that the main reason for denial was high blood pressure. I told her that I have always had very good blood pressure and I guaranteed that this would not be an issue. I asked her to recalibrate the percentage because I have great blood pressure, and she moved me into the 90s.

I was glad Teresa could not see me because several times, emotion took over and I was a visible mess. I tried not to speak during these moments as I am not sure words would have come out. As the reality of the moment sank in, I did not feel scared, unsure, or timid. I felt poised and assured that this was something I should do. I felt confident and did not second guess what I had gotten myself into.

Tears of relief were flowing for someone I barely remembered. Someone who was in desperate need of a kidney to sustain and nurture life, so she could live and raise her children. I was now in a position to help make that happen. This was the making of a miracle, and I would get to play a pretty big part in it.

I was driving during this entire conversation and I could clearly see a lot of smoke in the direction I was going. Santa Ana winds were gusting, which in Southern California means wildfires. I remember thinking I would be stuck for hours as it looked like the fire would engulf the freeway before I could get through. However, at this point in the conversation, the fire and I were intersecting at the same location. The fire was driving west, consuming everything in its path and I was speeding south on I-215 just north of Murrieta.

The fire was right alongside the freeway, and it felt like somebody opened the oven as I drove by. I could feel the extreme heat penetrating through my window and door. Teresa asked again that same piercing question from twenty minutes prior, "Would you like to proceed?" I lowered my foot on the car's accelerator and shot through the flames while I answered with an emphatic, "ABSOLUTELY!"

The conversation ended, and I was left to myself to think about what just happened. And what did just happen? I said yes to several more tests, a couple trips out of state, missing work for a month, the pain and recovery of major surgery, financial setback for my family, and hoping that my body could adjust for the rest of my life to one kidney. I just committed to giving away a solid organ.

Shouldn't I have done some research before I answered? Thought about it more? Prayed? Was I just caught up in the heat of the moment (literally)? No, I thought. I have had this feeling before, and it is unmistakable. I am doing the right thing.

I called Robin and told her everything. She was predictably surprised, then concerned about how I felt, and then overwhelmingly supportive. Wow, my wife. Clearly, I've done something right. Then I called Ozz. I told him I got a call from the transplant center with my test results. He asked, "What did they say?" I answered, "I'm the guy." There was disbelief, then relief that a donor had been found, and then more disbelief. He said, "I can't believe it, this is so awesome." I reminded him of the feeling he had, about him being the one to donate his kidney. I told him that what he felt was probably that he would be involved, even though it would be me on the table. Ozz asked me if the Petersens knew yet. I said that

23

the coordinator said that she thought they did. I asked Ozz if he thought I should reach out to them. He said to wait for them to contact me.

When our conversation ended, I could again see wildfire smoke in the direction I was driving, and I turned on the radio for an update. The fire that had nearly cooked me earlier was now being called the Liberty Fire. There was another fire that I could see now, the Bonsall (Lilac Fire) that looked and sounded much worse. As I got closer to that fire, still riding the emotions of the day, I experienced nearly the same thing as I had fewer than 30 minutes before: the jumping flames and extreme heat of the blaze, the fire consuming everything surrounding the freeway.

There is a false sense of security about being in a car. Once I drove by the towering red and orange flames and felt the scorching heat through the car doors, I realized how vulnerable I was. And I knew that those fire trucks and firefighters, planes and helicopters, couldn't do anything to stop the fire from tearing through the valley. Was God sending me a message? Was he sending it twice because I am not a good listener?

Today was a doozy. First, work sucked. Then, I felt ill. Immediately after that was the surreal experience of the kidney match phone call, during which I agreed to donate a kidney to save the life of someone I barely remember meeting. My wife's love and support were next; she was there for me, even though she had her hands full at home with our kids and their issues and special needs. Lastly, I experienced the kindness of a good brother, who originally thought that he would be the one to donate his kidney to help his friends. And now TWO FIRES!! SERIOUSLY??!

The intensity of the day's events and emotions coalesced. "OKAY, GOD!" I yelled out loud, "I GET IT!!" This is life! We love, we serve, we laugh, we cry, we feel pain, anguish, hardships, and we keep plugging along through the elements and fragile nature of mortal life. Grasp the magnitude of the Grace of God and the enormity of His unique plan for you! Next hour, there could be something more for you if you are aware of it and if you welcome the blessings it brings. If you can do that, then life in all of its facets is sweet.

December 8, 2017: Morning

Twilight Zone - Golden Earring

Wow. Did that really happen? Yesterday, I mean. Amazing experience? Check. Surreal? Check. And now I feel like I'm in that Chicken Little movie. It's the baseball scene, bottom of the 9th, two outs, bases loaded, and the championship game on the line. And there's me, Chicken Little, the only kid left on the bench, the one who the coach never imagined would see the batter's box. And yet there I am, forced to the plate with my draping uniform and borrowed bat, ill prepared for what is about to happen because I never thought this was possible.

December 8, 2017: Evening

The Simpsons Theme - Danny Elfman

That conversation with nurse Teresa yesterday was enlightening. Before we talked, most of what I knew about kidney donations came from the Simpsons. In the episode, Homer decided to give his dad one of his kidneys. But when the day came, Homer jumped from the operating table and escaped out the window the moment the doc turned his head. This happened twice. Pretty funny episode, especially since the second time Homer bolted, he got hit by a train. They brought him into the hospital (unconscious) and took his kidney. When Homer awoke, he saw his dad as healthy as could be and stitches in the outline of a kidney in his own side. Season 10, episode eight. Highly educational.

December 9, 2017

Leader of the Pack - Shangri Las

Today, I gathered Robin and the kids (Jefferson, 16; Ty 14; Jeremiah 12; Summer 7; Eli, 4) to get their input on my decision. I explained a little about human anatomy and about how all organs play their own roles. I said that sometimes parts become weak or fail and people can get sick and might even die. I explained that kidneys filter pee, regulate blood pressure, and control the production of red blood cells. I told them that most people have two kidneys but can function with just one. I said that each kidney is roughly the size of an adult fist. One of the kids chimed in, saying I was confused because the heart is the size of a fist. No, another piped up, bladder. No, stomach. Ah, families. Sometimes it's all about picking fights and being right.

I told them they were all correct and steered the conversation back to the kidneys. I explained that Uncle Ozz and Aunt Lindsey had a friend who needed one and that I was a suitable donor. The room got quiet, which is quite a remarkable achievement at our house. I then said that we were seriously considering doing this. The room stayed quiet—even more remarkable. I could see my kids' gears turning in their brains. I told them about the surgery, where it would take place, and that, if we did this, I would be away for about two weeks. I said that when it was done, I should be able to live exactly as I was living now.

I said that this was a family decision because it involved all of us, so we were not going to do it unless everyone was on board. I asked if anyone had any concerns or questions, wanted to talk more about it, or take some time to think. The replies came back, "cool, we're good." Just like that, I had full support from the whole family.

December 11, 2017

I'm Only One Call Away, I'll be There to Save the Day - Charlie Puth

As I mentioned a few days ago, Ozz thought it would be better if I waited for the Petersens to reach out to me. You never know, maybe they don't want my

27

kidney after all. Anyway, how does such a conversation go? "Hey, I'm Rick–you want a kidney?" Or, "Hey, Rick–you got something for me?"

Today, Ozz gave me a heads up that a phone call was coming. I was a little anxious, and I imagine the Petersens were too. When Steve called, I asked him a lot of questions about Jenny's health, their family's situation, and about the road to obtaining a kidney. That story was crazy! Steve told me about all the efforts of his and Jenny's extended family and friends to find a match. I asked him how they found out about me. I thought that the University of Utah Transplant Center had told them. Steve told me that the only thing the Center told them was that someone in California was a match, which made them scratch their heads because they could not figure out who it was.

Then Steve said that Ozz called him and said, "Fresh Ricky D saves the day!" Ha! That would be my rad street name from the 80s. And that is how they found out. He asked about how I even got on the list, the labs, and the steps I took. I told him everything, including my conversations with Nurse Teresa. We were really open with each other, and it was a pretty cool conversation.

I told Steve I had done a little research, discussed it with my family, and we were all on board. There was a long road ahead and we both knew it. But I told him I was ready to go. If I passed all the tests and got the green light, I was in; he did not have to worry about me bailing.

I asked Steve about future communication: Did he want me to report when I took a test or to keep it all to myself until we got the green light? Steve said that he and Jenny were open to whatever I was comfortable with. We discussed this for a while until I got a good sense of how they wanted to proceed. They wanted to be in the loop but were not going to pry for information. We ended the call on a good note. What I thought would be a dynamic conversation, really was. I felt good and ready to proceed.

I sent them an email a little later:

Communication
Rick Daynes
Mon 12/11/2017 10:40 AM

Hi Steve, since Jenny's name is in the address, I'll assume I am writing to both of you. HI JENNY! Steve and I had a great conversation earlier. I hope you are well. I also hope I'll pass the tests that are coming up and you'll get a healthy kidney soon. Robin and I are open to any communication either of you would like to have. Feel free to call, text, or email any time. As per my conversation with Steve, I will keep updating you on my progress unless you tell me otherwise.

Merry Christmas,
Rick Daynes

Jenny Petersen's reply:
Re: Communication
Steve & Jenny Petersen
Mon 12/11/2017 9:15 PM

Hi Rick and Robin!

We are truly in awe, completely humbled and amazed by your generous and kind hearts and willingness to do this for me. I know there is lots of testing yet to come, but whether you end up being the donor or not, I hope you will be greatly blessed for your willingness and desire to do this. Thank you seems so inadequate, but I hope you can feel the depth of my gratitude. I wish I could just go fix this on my own and not be dependent on someone else, and not need someone else to go through so much to help me. But as I can't, we find ourselves just completely overwhelmed, humbled and grateful for the extreme goodness in others (YOU!). We are so appreciative of both of you and recognize this is a decision that impacts your entire family. Thank you for being willing to take this step. It means everything to us.

Merry Christmas!
Jenny

December 11, 2017: Evening

She Blinded Me with Science - Thomas Dolby

Alright, let's face it. I don't know jack squat about kidneys. Well, maybe that's not true. A week ago, I did not know jack squat about kidneys. Now I know a little more than what I learned on the Simpsons. And I probably should know even more. So, I decided to read up and cover my bases.

Here's what I learned. Kidneys receive more blood than all other organs except the liver. Interesting. They regulate your blood pressure by adjusting the volume of blood in your circulatory system. Nephrons are the filtering units of the kidney. Cool! The kidneys have their own filtering units. Each kidney has between 1 to 2 million nephrons. Whoa, that's a lot of nephrons. So, if I give up a kidney, I might lose a million nephrons. Well, that is until my other kidney kicks in and produces more nephrons. Hmm, if I only knew what nephrons did...

Let's keep digging. Nephrons regulate the hormones that stimulate the production of red blood cells in bone marrow. Crazy! I did not know that bones made blood cells. Nephrons actually maintain many hormones that are vital to our existence. I guess this means I could have a hormonal imbalance with only one kidney. My wife might tell me (without sympathy), "Welcome to the club."

I sent the following email to my doctor:

From: RICHARD W DAYNES

Date: 12/11/2017 10:12 am

Subject: Kidney Donation

Hi Doc, I was contacted by the University of Utah on Thursday regarding blood work I sent in about a month ago. Turns out, I am number one on the list to donate a kidney to my brother's friend. I am educating myself on this process, but if you have anything to add, any suggestions, would like to see me, anything, just let me know.

Thanks,

Rick

He replied that he had a few other patients who were donors, and although this surgery was nothing to be taken lightly, it is usually safe. He said my kidney function (the Glomerular Filtration Rate or GFR) is on the low end of normal, but that shouldn't be an issue unless it gets lower. Plus, since I don't have hypertension, diabetes, or other medical issues, it would be OK to proceed. He said that the transplant team would do a battery of tests to make sure it was safe to go ahead and that he would also do a pre-op evaluation before the surgery.

December 14, 2017

What's Going On - Marvin Gaye

Nurse Teresa called today to go over my medical and surgical history. It's all part of the evaluation process. I learned more about the donation process, labs, and what to expect.

December 15, 2017

I Wonder, Wonder Who, Who Ooh Ooh, Who, Who Wrote the Book of Love? - The Monotones

Today, I was on a mission. I wanted to read a first-hand experience of someone who had donated. I was on a kidney quest and was hoping to get some guidance: the good, the bad, and the ugly. I wanted to hear about real experiences and I was glad to find several books on the subject.

I spent an hour reading book summaries and reviews. I considered several books but could not pull the trigger on any. Every book I opened had a religious theme. They were all stories about how God paved the way for the donation or performed a miracle.

It turned me off. Look, I consider myself a religious person. I believe in God, and I have no doubt that the people who authored those books had divine experiences. Shoot, I'm already having a spiritual experience with this. But why do all of the books have to be about divine intervention? Are only religious people donating kidneys? You're telling me no atheists or agnostics are giving up an organ? That can't be true.

The books weren't right for me because I was not searching for a religious experience. Why should God have to tell me to do something that is inherently selfless? Why should I depend on a deity to tell me to do something that is morally right? I am not saying that I do not want full approval and all the warm, fuzzy feelings and blessings from the man upstairs. I absolutely welcome that and I may need Him to get me through this. I'm just saying that if everyone waited to put themselves on the National Kidney Registry until God told them to, there would probably be a lot of unfortunate and seriously ill people. Current number of unfortunate people waiting for God to tell someone to donate to them: 120,000.

December 17, 2017

ABC, Easy as 1,2,3 - The Jackson Five

I emailed the Petersens an update:

Date: 12/17/2017

From: RICHARD W DAYNES

5:34 PM

Hi Steve and Jenny,

Thought I'd give you an update. I got a call from the U on Thursday. This was the most serious conversation to date. They took me through every step of the process, and it is pretty extensive. Looks like they test everything. Plus, classes, evaluation—basically, they cover all the ABCs and leave no stone unturned. Then, in the end, there is a panel that decides if I am eligible.

I usually ask a lot of questions during these conversations to get information they generally do not give out. From a mental, emotional, financial, social, and spiritual aspect, I'm good. I want you to know that Robin and I have not taken this lightly. We have prayed, gone to the temple, listened to doctors, educated ourselves, done the pros and cons, etc. And we are going to do this.

The woman I spoke with said that Jenny is not ready to get a transplant, and that they don't know when she will be ready–it could be a long time. She really emphasized this and said that there was no rush. From speaking to Steve, I know that is not the case.

Since it looks like the odds are in our favor, I decided to make my own plan, and here's how I see it. I want to get this done ASAP. Whether I pass the tests or not, I want to know now. The center is sending me another kit, and I hope to get that test done this week. If I pass that one, then I have a conference with a psychologist, a phone call or two, and then to the U for most testing. I believe at that point, it is in their court for a final verdict. Although there might be two visits to the U? I'm a little unsure.

The good news is that I know who my coordinator is and I have her phone number. So, I can follow up and move the process along faster. It may be premature to do a timeline, but I'm a bit of a planner and I like to have things mapped out when possible. So, I'm hoping to get a final green light from the U, hopefully in February.

I hope both of you are well and that your family is enjoying the Christmas season.

Rick

December 19, 2017

Steve's reply:

Re: Update

Tue 12/19/2017 6:08 AM

Rick and Robin,

We received your Christmas card in the mail a few days ago...thank you. You have a great-looking family, and congrats on getting the family picture done! You should be getting one from us shortly as well.

We appreciate the update on your discussions with the U! On the one hand, we are grateful that the testing for a donor is so thorough and comprehensive from a donor safety perspective...on the other hand, we hope it isn't overwhelming and overly time consuming! Jenny gets her kidney function and a panel of other labs tested every four weeks and got her results back last week. Jenny's kidney function stayed at 13%, which is positive news. We are so grateful that, even with a kidney function of 13%, Jenny is able to carry out her normal mom duties, run the house, etc., and generally feels pretty good (except for needing to nap once in a while).

The "when" discussion is multi-dimensional, and I was hoping maybe to chat on the phone to discuss. Too much to write in an email. Maybe when you have 15 minutes, you can give me a call.

All the best to la familia Daynes! We hope you have a Merry Christmas!

Steve and Jenny

December 19, 2017: Afternoon

You May be Wrong but You May be Right - Billy Joel

My first bit of opposition came today. He had been hinting about it earlier but came straight out with it today. My dad, Mr. Optimistic, does not want me to do this. He said, "Rick, you are going to heaven already because you got Eli [my son with Down syndrome]. You don't need to do this." Hilarious. My dad thinks I am donating my kidney so I can get into heaven.

This, actually, is not surprising. Everything is spiritual with my dad, so that statement is pretty much in keeping with his thought process as to why his son would give up a kidney. Of course, I had not thought about a kidney donation being my ticket to the pearly gates. But now that he mentioned it, I guess it doesn't hurt. I told my dad that the woman I am donating my kidney to has four kids, including one with Down Syndrome. She has a lot of people depending on her and I wanted her to be around for a long time. I also said, "Dad, plus her husband is a total dead beat and has no idea how to take care of their kids, so we gotta do this!" We both laughed. He knew that wasn't true.

I was really surprised at how my dad persisted in trying to talk me out of donating. He finally said, "before you decide to do this, you need to talk to Uncle Randy [my dad's brother and a doctor]." Just to get off the phone with him, I promised to call Uncle Randy, which I did the second I hung up with my dad.

Uncle Doctor Randy had been talking with my dad and knew my call was coming. He basically said that he was not worried about how I would do now with donating. However, he was worried about my health several years down the road. He told me that his kidneys were in decline and that I would need both of mine when I got older. He said, "You better be really sure you are supposed to do this." I told him I was and that was the extent of our talk.

I rang my dad back and stated I had done what he wanted. I told him I understood their concerns, but that I did not want him to bring it up again. Believe me, he will anyway; that's what he does.

I was annoyed with my dad and my uncle, especially my dad. I understood their concerns and I appreciated them both for bringing up the downside to donating. They both love me and want what's best. Still, it was my decision, and I was annoyed.

December 19, 2017: Evening

Talking in Your Sleep - The Romantics

Pillow talk with Robin tonight after we got the kids to bed featured today's conversation with my dad and Uncle Doctor Randy (or is it Doctor Uncle Randy? Hmm?). I did some extra research after speaking with them, and I couldn't find anything that suggested they were right. All the information I found said that I would live a long, healthy life with one kidney.

Still, I couldn't help thinking, "What if I don't? What if I have complications down the road?" I have good to great genes. One of my grandfathers died unexpectedly at 97 and the other at 102. My grandmothers passed away at 89 and 98. So, I expect to be in that ballpark. Still. Say I make it to 95 years old with two kidneys and only to 85 with one. Would I give 10 years of my life in my 80s and 90s so a woman could be healthy enough to raise her four kids today? Absolutely. Would I give 20 years of my life so she could be healthy enough to live and raise her kids to adulthood? No-brainer. What will I be doing from age 75 to 95 that is more important than Jenny teaching and raising a family? Let's see, maybe I'll take up golf? Walking? Annoying my grandkids with stories of the good ole days? If out of the blue, I happen to die because of anything related to kidneys, then this is the story that my grandkids will hear at my funeral. "Grandad died a little early because he gave his kidney to someone who needed it more." I could only be so lucky. AND. I just found this out and it's pretty cool. If a kidney donor needs a kidney, they go straight to the front of the line. Finally, by the time I might need a kidney, there will probably be an artificial one perfected and ready to roll. No problemo.

December 20, 2017

You're So Vain - Carly Simon

The University of Utah Medical Center sent more lab work orders to the lab in San Diego. I went in to have the lab work done, but it took forever. Because the orders came from an outside facility and things had to be verified, people had to figure out who was paying for what, etc. Same thing that happened last time except this time, nobody was out to lunch. They were on vacation.

Christmas was days away, and people were taking time off, going to office parties, etc. So, the woman in the lab could not get in touch with anyone in Utah to verify the orders.

Finally, my favorite lab tech, Mr. Stick, came out. I was like, "Come on man, let's do this thing." He said, "Bruh, pump the brakes, We'll get you in there after all the Ts have been crossed." Enter Nurse Goodtidings to save the day! My doctor's office is on the same floor as the lab, just down the hall. So, Stick reached out to my doctor to see if he could verify the labs and get me stuck. Of course, my doc was not there because... who knows why? But let's be real here. It's undoubtedly related to Christmas.

No matter, Goodtidings is in my doctor's office! She sees the issue and makes a couple calls, waves her magic wand in the air, and next thing I know, Mr. Stick is probing for a vein.

You know when you get labs drawn and they bring in one or two vials to be filled? The tech labels each vial to be tested for something? Well, when you are taking labs for a potential kidney donation, they bring in a couple cords of vials. Seriously, I'm sitting in the chair and Stick pours all these vials onto a cookie sheet like my son empties his Legos onto a metal coffee table. Same sound too. Makes you jump if you don't know what's happening.

I filled those tubes pretty quickly. Still, when there are that many, it takes a while. Stick and I discussed our holiday plans. I found out that he's getting his wife a diamond upgrade on her engagement ring and that he's pretty sure there will be a new grill under the tree for him. He's hoping it's not a George Foreman.

With all the vials filled Christmas red and my face a Grinchy green, I ventured to the bathroom with the usual specimen cup for my last deposit of the day. Everything went fluidly, and I was out the door with two bottles of water, courtesy of the Stick Man.

From what I understand, these labs are a huge part of the process. They test for in-depth kidney function and other things relating to my overall health. This is the clincher that will decide if I'm the guy.

I'm excited. I had pushed Nurse Teresa to expedite these orders. When they arrived at the lab, I made sure I had the first appointment this morning. And while the Stick Man was doing his thing, I asked him if they could rush the results. Stick knows the tests are for a kidney donation, so he's all in. I told him if they could pull off the results by tomorrow, it would be part of a Christmas miracle.

December 21, 2017

Let's Go Crazy - Prince and the Revolution

I sent the following email to the Petersens:

Update 12/21
Thu 12/21/2017 8:54 AM

Hi Friends,

I did all my lab work yesterday. Pretty sure I am completely done with lab stuff. Also filled out paperwork and had it notarized and sent back. I then called and emailed my coordinator with all the updates and asked for a list of everything left. Basically told her I would like to get crackin on this stuff.

I think today is huge as we should get the results from yesterday's labs. Just got to pass those last labs! So, prayers for that. Other than that, the only thing I am worried about is my clinic day when they look at my kidneys. Below is the email my coordinator sent to me. It is exactly what I asked for, a list of everything I have left. And it's all soon. Nothing but good news and positive vibes. I hope everyone has a spring in their step today!

Rick

Taking Care of Business - Bachman Turner Overdrive

From: Nurse Teresa
Date: 12/21/2017 9:20 am
Subject: Steps

Rick,

Here are the next steps of the process:

1. Attend the Living Donor Education class via telephone. You are scheduled for Tuesday, December 26th at 1:00 PM MST. The PowerPoint presentation was sent in your initial packet.

2. I will review your lab results with our team and let you know if we need any additional testing.

3. Psychosocial evaluation. This will be done over the phone with Caprice, our Living Donor Social Worker. After you have completed education, I will have her contact you to set up a time.

4. Come to Clinic. Clinic is on Wednesdays from 9 AM to 1 PM. This includes appointments with a nephrologist, transplant surgeon, dietician, and social worker. You will also get a chest X-ray and we will look at your heart rhythm and your kidney anatomy.

If your lab results look good and we don't need further testing, we can schedule your clinic appointment. Right now, I have January 3rd, January 10th, January 17th, and January 24th available.

I will be available tomorrow morning if you have further questions. Otherwise, I will call you after I have reviewed your lab results.

It's the Most Wonderful Time of the Year - Andy Williams

Today is Thursday (still 12/21). I found out yesterday (Wednesday) that all the health offices would be closed on Friday. I mean, why should anyone have to work the Friday before Christmas!? Never mind that Christmas day isn't until Monday! Anything to make it a four-day weekend, I guess. That is why I felt the urgency to get my labs drawn yesterday and hopefully obtain the results today. I did not have to ship anything back to Utah. It's all being done in-house, here in my town. Since deciding I was going to do this kidney thing, I figured, might as well get it done ASAP.

I mean, there is a woman who is in desperate need. There is a family who has been through the ringer.

All of Jenny and Steve's family members got checked out and none were compatible. Are you kidding me? I thought of all their friends who were willing to help, and none passed the test. Now, their prayers are finally answered as they get word that someone is a match. Then comes the news that it is someone they may have met once who lives 1,000 miles away in Southern California, a brother of a friend. Their hope, their future, rests with a guy they do not even know. They don't know if I might flake out or what is going through my brain.

Because of all the things the Petersens have gone through—the things I know, don't know, and can only imagine—I really want to give them a kidney for Christmas. This next part might actually be more for me than them: I want to email them one of those Christmas Cards with the ridiculous dancing elves and write, "Merry Christmas Petersen Family. I passed my last blood and urine tests with flying colors. I am ready to go. I have never done this before, but I think the rest of the testing and visits might simply be a formality. Please have a Merry Christmas. Love, the Daynes." Wouldn't that be cool?

So, today's the day! The labs and offices are closed tomorrow through Monday, Monday being Christmas. If I don't get results today, there will be no kidney under the Petersens' tree. I shot Nurse Goodtidings an email this morning:

From: RICHARD W DAYNES
Date: 12/21/2017 10:03 am
Subject: RE: Labs

Hi Nurse Goodtidings, Thanks for helping me out yesterday. Could you do me a favor? When my labs come back, would you see that they are posted on Follow My Health? I'm a little anxious to see them.

Thanks,

Rick

You're Unbelievable - EMF

THIS IS FREAKING UNBELIEVABLE! I am recording this right after I sent Nurse Goodtidings that email and had a conversation with Robin that totally floored me! As I've mentioned, our five-year-old son, Eli, has Down Syndrome; he also has Autism. We found out about the Down Syndrome during Robin's pregnancy.

It is difficult to describe how we felt when we found out that our unborn child had Down Syndrome. Robin was having a horrific pregnancy and had taken the test to find out if our baby had Trisomy 21 (Down Syndrome). I was eager to get the negative test results back because I needed some good news to brighten my sick wife's life. I called Robin's Ob-Gyn and asked for the test results.

When I spoke with the nurse, she was being a little vague and acting somewhat strange. She was not allowed to tell me the disappointing results of the Trisomy test. I figured it out anyway. This was such a poignant moment. It is the genesis of my book "Keep It Together Man, for Dads with a Special Kid." The detailed story of that interaction with the nurse is on the opening pages.

Well, Robin just informed me that her Ob-Gyn nurse of almost six years ago IS THE ONE AND ONLY NURSE GOODTIDINGS! The very same nurse who saved the day for me yesterday. I immediately shot her another email:

From: RICHARD W DAYNES
Date: 12/21/2017 10:15 am
Subject: YOU!

Goodtidings! My wife Robin just said to me, "Can you believe Goodtidings works for our doctor now?" WHATTT!!!!!! I cannot believe that was you yesterday and I never put it together! Do you remember our phone conversation six years ago when you did not tell me we were expecting a child with Down Syndrome, but I figured it out anyway? That conversation changed our lives forever! and that was YOU! I cannot tell you how many good tidings of great joy we have received because of that kid. And you've helped Robin so much!

Thanks!
Rick

December 21, 2017: Afternoon

Time Warp - The Rocky Horror Picture Show

Every passing hour of this day, I am more anxious than the hour before. The morning came and went with no response regarding the labs. I was checking the clock constantly. When lunch rolled around with no call, my chances of getting my test results today began to diminish. My afternoon was completely non-productive. All I did was stare at the clock, which soon became my nemesis. I started having conversations with it. I said, "Look, I have already emailed the nurse, twice. I called and left a message once. Don't you think that is enough? She knows I am waiting for the results. Don't you believe in Christmas miracles? Don't you think this would warrant a small Christmas miracle? If we don't get the results back in the next few hours, that's it! No kidney under the tree. Wouldn't it be nice if they could have a relaxing Christmas, knowing that a kidney was all but secure and a transplant was in the near future?"

I kept my body busy, an eye on the clock, and hope in my heart. 2:00 turned to 3:00. Are my results just sitting in an endless stack of electronic files on someone's desk? I was sure they were. 4:00 was the hour I assumed everyone would go home. It's a four-day weekend and I'm sure they were all calling it quits early today. 4:00 approached and I resumed my staring competition with the clock. Frustrated, I resorted to talking smack to it. It was the natural progression of my frustration.

4:00 sauntered by without incident. I prayed. I apologized to the clock for my insulting remarks. I held out hope for 5:00.

5:00 snickered by annoyingly, like a little brat sticking his tongue out at me. The offices were closed. There would be no Christmas miracle this year. My lab results were probably done and sitting somewhere, calling for me, but to no avail. Probably because whoever was supposed to input the results needed to get some last-minute Christmas shopping done. I resorted back to smack talking the clock and went about the rest of my day, irritated.

I continued to monitor my email that evening. While transferring my kids to their sports practices at 6:15, I glanced at my phone and was stunned to see I had two messages from my doctor's office!

From: The Office of MD
To: RICHARD W DAYNES
Date: 12/21/2017 5:59 pm
Subject: RE: YOU!

Hi Richard, yes, I do remember the conversation and I am so happy that little one has made your lives so full–I actually got to see pictures a few years ago when I was working the RB office and saw Robin–and then I got to see Robin not too long ago. :) Nurse Goodtidings

From: The Office of MD
To: RICHARD W DAYNES
Date: 12/21/2017 6:14 pm
Subject: RE: Labs

Hi Richard, I can mail the results to you if you like but we cannot add them to Follow My Health since they were from an outside provider–let me know.

Goodtidings

From: RICHARD W DAYNES
Date: 12/21/2017 6:16 pm
Subject: RE: RE: RE: Labs

Can I pick them up?

From: The Office of MD
To: RICHARD W DAYNES
Date: 12/21/2017 6:33 pm
Subject: RE: RE: RE: Labs

Yes, you can pick them up. Do you want to wait until
the labs you had done yesterday are back and pick all
of them up at once?

Goodtidings

From: RICHARD W DAYNES
Date: 12/21/2017 6:46 pm
Subject: RE: RE: RE: RE: RE: Labs

Yes! Thanks, Rick

From: The Office of MD
To: RICHARD W DAYNES
Date: 12/21/2017 6:53 pm
Subject: RE: RE: RE: RE: RE: Labs

They are ready for pick up now–looks like they came
in already–we are here til 7:30pm tonight.

Goodtidings

I emailed and said I would be there before 7:30 PM,
even though Google Maps said the earliest I could get
there was 7:41.

After ditching some kids and breaking a few traffic
laws, I sprinted into the doctor's office and arrived at
7:34. The offices were all dark. I ran to the lab down

the hall and found a receptionist packing up for the night. She told me that everyone had gone home. I asked her if she would please call back into my doctor's office just to see if anyone was there. She picked up the phone, let it ring for a while and then said, "I'm sorry sir, everyone in the doctor's office has gone home for the night."

I could not believe I had missed it. I stood there, totally dejected. A security guard down the hall beckoned me to exit the building as it was past closing time. Only a few lights were still on, and it was clear we were the only three people on the floor. The receptionist continued to gather her things and she looked at me as if to ask, "What are you still doing here, looking around like you lost your mommy?"

I just could not move. I don't know why. I guess I was trying to milk a few more seconds, and for what? The security guard was walking toward me, no doubt to escort me out. I took one last look in the direction of my doctor's office and turned to the exit. I began walking and the security guard nodded his approval and held out his arm showing me the way out.

"Wait!" I heard a voice behind me say. I turned around and there was Nurse Goodtidings with papers in her hand! I could not believe my luck. I yelled out, "It's a Christmas miracle!" This made the lab receptionist and security guard laugh. Goodtidings handed me my lab results. I said, "You saved the day yet again!"

I looked at the paper containing my lab results and thanked her profusely. I was over the moon with excitement and optimism. That is until I realized I had no idea how to decipher the medical jargon on the pages. I asked, "Now, how the heck am I supposed to know what any of this means?" She said, "Let me take a look." Then she pointed out the GFR and some of the stand-out numbers. She told me that everything looked good to her but there were some things she was unsure of. She said, "What you really need, to be sure, is for a nephrologist to read this."

I asked, "What's a nef-a-ump-a-gist?" Which came out sounding more like Snuffleupagus than nephrologist. She said, "It's a kidney doctor." "Kidneys have their own doctors?" I questioned. "Sure do," she replied. I couldn't help but laugh inside. I have heard that word a couple times, but like most times, when I don't recognize a word, I just move on. This word will undoubtedly be an important one moving forward. So, I'm putting it in the old vault.

I left the office elated, but with a new problem on my hands. When I got home, I shared the good news with Robin. She took a look at my labs and said the same thing Nurse Goodtidings did. However, I was amazed how much she knew. What looked like pages of chicken scratch to me, she easily clarified. Chalk up another benefit to being married to a nurse.

December 21, 2017: Evening

It's Beginning to Look a Lot Like Christmas - Meredith Willson

We got a Christmas card from the Petersen family today. You will recall that I did meet them. It's been a while. Four and a half years now. I do remember meeting them and having a brief conversation. Well.

Maybe I don't remember as well as I thought I did. On the card is a picture of a beautiful family and they look nothing like the picture in my head. Huh.

I called Ozz and told him that we received a Christmas card from the Petersens. He had received one as well. I asked if Jenny had dyed her hair. He said, nope. I told him, "I thought she had blond hair. And Steve does not look anything like I remember. I don't remember the kids, except Jon. Oh well, no biggie. Merry Christmas."

It was quite a day.

December 22, 2017

Don't Go Breaking My Heart - Elton John

Today was one of those days. I knew I should be doing something, but I just could not pull the trigger. You see, I really needed a nephrologist to read my labs and I actually know one (I'm getting better at spelling that word, but it still sounds like snuffleupagus to me). Okay, maybe I don't really know him, but he has a daughter who is friends with my son. Also, he has an adorable daughter with Down Syndrome, so he is totally in my club! Still, I couldn't reach out, even though I knew he would have helped me out. Luckily, I have Robin. And between her and Doctor Google, we were fairly certain my labs were in the good range.

I called Steve Petersen and told him the good news. I had the results of my labs and according to Nurses Robin and Goodtidings, they looked good. No red flags anyway. The conversation was not exactly what I had rehearsed in my mind, but the kidney was under the tree. However, because there were too many items on the spreadsheet that we weren't sure about, my excitement was quelled.

The Petersens are friendly yet guarded. My phone conversations with Steve are fun and we are getting to know each other, but Steve and especially Jenny are not going to get one inch ahead of themselves. I thought about how many heartbreaks they must have had just in the last year. The Petersens will not be celebrating an available kidney until it's in a silver bowl next to Jenny on the operating table. I can't say I blame them.

December 23, 2017

Ain't No Stoppin' Us Now - McFadden & Whitehead

Now that I'm in—I mean, I'm guessing I'm in the mid to high 90s as far as probability that this donation goes through, right? By all accounts, I passed the major lab work. The psych evaluation is a no-brainer. They still need to look at my kidneys and make sure I indeed have two of them. There is that. A lot of people have one kidney and don't know it. They also need to pick which one they want to seize. I think they typically favor extracting the left one. Other than that, what else is there? So, now that I'm in, I'm thinking there ain't no stopping us now.

During one of my interviews with Nurse Teresa, she mentioned that I needed to tell my family that all systems were go. Well, I am at that point. I don't anticipate any problems with my family, as I am sure they will all be in full support. Even my dad is on board, though maybe not fully. I drafted the following email and sent it out to my family and Robin's.

From: RICHARD W DAYNES
Date: 12/23/2017 6:43 am
Subject: Got Kidney?

Dear Family,

Quick story. O&L have sweet friends, the Petersens. You may have met them as they came to San E with them twice. They have four kids, one with Down Syndrome. At DFR Paradise, Lindsey told me that Jenny, the mom, needed a kidney. They had searched both sides of the family and had not found a match. I asked Lindsey to forward me the link to sign up, which she did, and I signed up.

After the search went through O&L, the ward, congregation, and community, they broadened the search to outsiders in other states. Let's check this dude out with the O- blood in San Diego. And you guessed it, I'm a match. In the last two months, I have done more lab work than Dr. Bunsen Honeydew. This includes the Steve Daynes 24-hour urine test, the drink a bottle of sugar and draw blood every hour to see how your body handles it, psych evaluations, interviews, and on and on. And I continue to nail every exam! If only I had done this well in school.

Robin and I have prayed, been to the temple, prayed, educated ourselves, prayed, talked to Uncle Randy and other doctors, and considered, hashed up, and dissected every worst- and best-case scenario.

Contrary to what Dad thinks, I don't go driving around everyday looking for someone to save. Bottom line is, Robin and I feel great about this and have had several spiritual experiences that confirm our decision.

Currently, Jenny has one kidney functioning at 13% so I have been trying to get through the testing ASAP. I have one more test to pass. It's at the U, probably Jan 10. They will look at my kidneys and all of my organs. Chances of passing this test are very good, but you never know. A panel will then meet, review everything, and (I hope) give me the green light. Then we stand in the on-deck circle waiting for Jenny and her doctors to tell us we are up. Could happen soon and it could happen... in six months... longer... echo... echo...

My psychologist tells me that I must inform you that down the road, I will be five to ten times more likely to develop kidney disease. And I will have a higher chance of developing other health problems, including a hernia! Yes! Been waiting for that one all my life. And I will be ostracized to the shire to live among my new peers of one-kidney hobbits. You can help with love, prayers, and support for both families involved. We have faith and know the Lord is in charge.

KIT,

Rick

December 26, 2017

I took a kidney class today. They sent me a PowerPoint presentation and we went over it. Living Kidney Donor Education Class. Check. Easy peasy.

January 3, 2018

Would I Lie to You? - Eurythmics

The results are finally in! Got a call from Nurse Teresa at the University of Utah Transplant Center this morning. Looks like everyone is now home from Christmas vacation and ready to get to work. I asked what her people thought of my test results from, I don't know…12 days ago? She said they looked fine, but there was something they wanted to test again. Hmmm. I asked her what they wanted to retest for. Did I fail something? She said no, I didn't fail anything, but I was in the gray area on something and the doctors just want to make certain everything is 100%. Although our conversation was brief, I could clearly sense that Teresa was trying to smooth over a bad result.

Teresa found another agency to do the retesting and sent me there. I figured it wouldn't take long and I jumped in the car and headed in. But I couldn't shake this feeling I had. Why 12 days to get the results? Why send me to another agency to get tested instead of my doctor's lab? The whole thing smelled of failure.

When I arrived at the lab, I was surprised to see a hole in the wall joint in a strip mall. I went in and they already had the orders from the Transplant Center.

Then it was on: the usual spread of half a dozen vials on a tray. A plastic tray. So, is this place cheaper because they went with plastic trays over metal trays? Or does the sound from the metal tray drive everyone nuts? Hmm. There were way less vials than the last time, which was good because the stick is starting to get to me a little. But I've got the routine down now. Rubber rope around my arm, stick, bleed, fill, bandage, bathroom, deposit, and I am out the door.

I'm pretty sure today was my first semi-serious setback. But I'll pass the test and it'll all be good.

January 8, 2018

Honestly - Kelly Clarkson

Since we are being honest here, let's continue with the uncomfortable theme. One of the funniest stories in my family was during high school when my little brother had to collect his urine throughout a 24-hour period. I was out of the house when this happened. However, just the thought of my teenage brother keeping his urine in the fridge is side splitting. And everyone having to look at it when they opened the fridge is hilarious.

Well, now it's my turn. Actually, it's my second 24-hour urine test in this donation process. The Transplant Center wants me to do it again as part of retaking the labs. So here we go. Let's do the urine test again. YES!

I woke yesterday with great anticipation for the day. Who wouldn't be excited about peeing in a jug all day? First pee of the day is in your toilet, but the rest of the day, your urination station is wherever you are. It's portable. In fact, I think we're on to something here. You have to keep it cool, so I carried it around in a cooler with some ice. Everyone thought it was my lunch. I couldn't wait for someone to ask me what I was having.

The most important thing is to preserve every drop of urine you produce over those 24 hours. Timing bathroom breaks is crucial because you have to be in a secluded location. One guy gave me a quizzical look when he saw me taking my cooler into a public bathroom. The highlight of the day was bringing it home and putting it in the fridge. I could have worked my way around this, but the thought of my kids opening up the fridge, craving some apple juice, was too funny to pass up.

Unfortunately, Robin put her foot down and squashed my juvenile antics. Sadly, I moved my pee back to the cooler. OH! I can't believe I forgot this. You have to record the time on the jug every time you relieve yourself. So, yeah. Good times for all. Seriously, it was pretty funny though. I turned that beer mug in this morning more than half full. That's the optimist in me.

January 11, 2018

Let's Go Crazy – Prince

From: Rick Daynes

Sent: Thursday, January 11, 2018 5:41 AM

To: Nurse Teresa

Subject: lab results

Hi Nurse Teresa,

Any word on my lab results? I have a physical scheduled with my doctor this afternoon. If there is something wrong with my kidneys or anything else, I would love to know so I can discuss with him.

Thanks,

Rick Daynes

From: Teresa
Sent: Thursday, January 11, 2018 8:23 AM
To: Rick Daynes
Subject: RE: lab results

Rick,

I do have the results and would like to talk to you about them. I just tried calling you. Please call me when you get a minute.

Notes from my call with Teresa:

Teresa and I talked about progress and setbacks. My labs are not quite where they want them to be. I again asked if this was a failing thing. She again downplayed it. Or maybe downplay is not the word. I'm still in the game, right? Teresa told me again that some things were elevated in my labs. Not sure what, but I need to take them again.

My next labs will be at the University of Utah. They want me on their home court to do them. These won't be any old labs. This is a test to end all tests. It has a distinct name: Iothalamate. Teresa says it's the "gold standard" of kidney tests. This will be the ultimate decider. I do the test on February 9th; apparently, it takes hours. Why would it take hours? I guess we'll find out. If I pass my test, sorry—WHEN I pass the test, I will have my clinic day on Wednesday. Wednesday is huge as it's the day I meet all the major players, and see where and how everything happens, and I think an X-ray or two? Basically, it's the last step.

From: Rick Daynes

Sent: Thursday, January 11, 2018 11:06 AM

To: Steve and Jenny Petersen

Cc: Ozz Daynes

Subject: Update 1/11

Morning!

FINALLY got the results from round two. Results are that some things that looked bad previously look fine now. However, other results are still inconclusive. My coordinator assures me that this is common. Long story short, they need me to come in to take an Iothalamate test. It's a four-hour test and must be done on a Friday. So, this is what I am scheduled for Friday, Feb 9th 8:30 AM lab testing at the U. We should get the results by Tuesday Feb 13th. If I pass, I go to my scheduled clinic appointment the next day, Wednesday, Feb 14th 9:00 AM, Clinic day at the U.

I am planning on doing this in one trip. Hold off on booking any flights. I am hoping to get my psych evaluation done and have my application sent into that organization that helps guys like me with travel.

Hope you both are well,

Rick

From: Steve Petersen <steve.jenny@gmail.com>
Sent: Thursday, January 11, 2018 2:07 PM
To: Rick Daynes
Cc: Ozz Daynes
Subject: Re: Update 1/11

Rick,

Thanks for the update! We are sorry to hear that lab tests continue...sort of an onerous process.

This morning, Jenny got the results back from her latest round of lab tests, and her kidney function declined from 13% to 12%...despite it being a decline, we are grateful it wasn't a big drop.

We are cognizant and sensitive to the fact that being gone Thursday the 8th through Wednesday the 14th is a big imposition on you and your family. We would be glad to pay for you to fly in on Thursday night, and home Friday night, and then for you to come back on Tuesday or Wednesday of the next week depending on how flights work out. It's more time in the airport/airplane that way, but at least you get a feel for what Ozz is doing each week and can be more empathetic to him. :) Really, we are happy to cover the multiple flights if it reduces the burden on you and your family.

Let me know if there is a portion of the application that we need to complete, and we'll get it turned around quickly.

We appreciate so much your willingness to go down this road. Throughout this process we've wished we could see the end from the beginning but acknowledge that it doesn't work that way. We are so grateful to you for your willingness to take this journey with us.

All the best,

Steve

January 11, 2018: Afternoon

Bad Moon Rising - Creedence Clearwater Revival

Today I went to see my doctor for a physical, just to make sure I was good to go. Doc's like, "You're at that age when we should check your prostate." I said, "No Doc, we're good on that." He started telling me of guys he had saved because of early detection. He is a good doctor, has to be, right? Why would anyone want to check that? And why would anyone be so persistent when I kept asking for a pass?

So, there you have it. It was so lame, I can't even joke about it. So, so lame. And when I'm 50, I get a colonoscopy. So, I've got that to look forward to. Whoo hoo!

I passed the physical with flying colors. Doctor Jellyfinger says I'm healthy and he has no issues with the kidney donation. We went over labs: no red flags. Only docs that are seeing red (or orange?) flags are the docs at the Transplant Center. Those are the guys that count. Nevertheless, all systems go for me per Doc Jelly!

It's My Life - Bon Jovi

I am a goal guy. I have always been. I just wrote down all my goals for this year and let's just say I went light. Or is it heavy? Normally, I write several goals under half a dozen categories. This year, I wrote down one central goal: Donate my kidney. I included two supplemental goals: lose 10 pounds and be in shape for the surgery.

I made only one central goal for two reasons. One, I cannot ever remember obtaining 100% of my annual goals. Maybe I'm a little inattentive with them? (I think I need to do better with this). Second, donating a kidney is a pretty big deal. If I donate a kidney this year, shouldn't everything else be gravy? If I accomplished nothing else this year except giving a kidney to save someone's life, wouldn't that be a pretty good year?

63

January 11, 2018: Evening

Papa Don't Preach – Madonna

OK, it's still the same day, the 11th of January and I need to vent. There's just so many thoughts, so many obscure to punch-in-the-gut emotions that happened over the last couple of weeks. First off, I'm getting sick of my dad. He's always sure to remind me that I don't need to donate. He's not a bad guy. It's just that every time we talk, the first thing he says is something about how I should not be doing this, or how I should really think about it, or something negative, which is really surprising because he's a pretty positive guy.

I emailed my family and got nothing but great supportive responses from both my and Robin's side of the family. That is, with one exception. So, in yet another conversation with my dad, he asked if I had run this by my Bishop? And I was like, uh, no. He was really surprised that I had not done that. Not sure why. It's not high on my priority list. I guess I knew that I would at some point, but it did not seem like a big deal to me. My dad is totally fishing for someone, other than himself, to object to this. So, he's telling me to run this by my church leaders and he's hoping that someone will talk some sense into me.

To appease him, I said "okay, I'll let my leaders know." But I was really thinking, if you think any of them are going to tell me this is a bad idea, then get ready for disappointment.

I forwarded the same family email to my bishop and a few others, including two doctor friends.

Opposites Attract - Paula Abdul

So, here I've got my dad telling me that what I'm doing is a bad idea, but my mom (Jane) thinks it is a great idea. She has actually been pretty cool about all of it. And she is not just sayin' it. She went to the National Kidney Registry to put her name on the list. As you can imagine, when you put your name on the list, there is a screening process followed by health history and a few items. Unfortunately, my mom did not make it past the first page of the screening form because of her age. But how cool is that?! My mom, trying to give away a kidney! If only she had been successful in getting on the list, it would have been priceless to see my dad's reaction. And that's where we are right now. January 11th. For those of you keeping score at home: Mom, cool. Dad, not cool.

January 14, 2018

People Are People – Depeche Mode

The folks from the Transplant Center say not to be shy about letting people know you are on the road to donation. I believe the reason is to gain support. I'm not really ready to post on Facebook: "HEY EVERYBODY! LOOK AT ME! I'M GOING TO DONATE A KIDNEY!" I don't even know how that comes up in casual conversations with friends? Friend: "Hey Rick, how's it going?" Me: "Great, I'm trying to lose some weight and I found someone who will take a kidney." Hmm.

So, who *have* I told? Immediate family: Check. It's been fun talking about this with Robin and our kids. Extended family: Check. Opposition from my dad and Uncle Doctor Randy: Annoying. Everyone else is cool. Close friends? Not yet, but I'm sure it'll come up one day. Work peeps? Nope. Religious leaders? I do have great church leaders, but I wasn't planning on involving them until my dad got on my case. So I sent them the following, and also included the same email I sent to my family on December 23.

Dear Church Leaders,

I have something on the horizon and figured I should probably let my priesthood leaders know, especially since one of you is a doctor. See below. It is an email I sent my family a couple weeks ago.

Happy Sunday!

Rick

This email went to four friends in my church. Everyone replied affirmatively, but one response really surprised me. One of my leaders is also a doctor. He and I spoke in the parking lot after church. I thought he had some physical advice for me, but surprisingly, he was all about...wait for it....

the money.

He said, "Rick, it's not unreasonable to ask for money. You go in there and you say, 'Look, I'm going to donate a kidney, right? This is my part. I'm donating a kidney. But I'm going to miss a significant amount of work.' It's not unreasonable for you to ask for money."

He's such a good guy and I'm sure he's looking out for me. But I was really scratching my head over his response. Money? Ask the recipient for money? He's not advising me to sell my kidney. He's just saying, "you'll lose a couple weeks of work and should be compensated." I never expected a response like that. I kept telling him, "We're gonna be fine." And we are going to be fine. Plus, I'm pretty darn sure asking for money is against the law.

Maybe he thinks we are in financial distress? I don't think so. But I would never dream of asking for money. It's so ridiculous and makes me so uncomfortable to even think about it or write it down. But I'm recording everything. People are people and I'm sure I'll get plenty more surprises.

January 20, 2018

Is Anybody Out There? - Def Leppard

I have been thinking that I would really like to talk to a donor. Preferably, someone I know. You know, get it first hand. I was also curious to see if I knew anyone who had donated, so I asked on Facebook if I had any friends who had donated a kidney.

Five people replied, saying either that a cousin or friend had done it. Kind of disappointing. Then I got a response from a guy I went to high school with. I did not remember this guy well, but it was good to hear that I at least had one FB friend who donated a kidney. It was to his brother. I messaged him and we had a brief but cool conversation about it. Not a lot of details, just that he was in good health and had no regrets. I suppose that's all I needed to hear.

January 23, 2018

Comfortably Numb – Pink Floyd

I had my psych evaluation today. I believe the technical term, just to cross it off my list, is "Social Work Evaluation." Of course, I nailed it. I told the therapist I had already told my family and religious leaders about the donation. She asked why I did not share the good news with more people, and I told her I didn't see the need. No hard questions, all in all, not a big deal. Easy peasy lemon squeezy.

January 24, 2018

Money Changes Everything - Cyndi Lauper

Money. Ah yes, the money. One of the awkward necessities of kidney donation. I am not a rich man, but my family and I are comfortable. I was willing to donate a kidney and endure the time, loss of work, education, and testing to get it done. Robin and I also talked about the travel and lodging expenses and determined that we were likely okay covering this as well.

We did find out that there was an organization called the National Living Donor Assistance Center that provided travel and lodging to living donors like me, and I thought contacting them would be a good idea.

The Transplant Center had me fill out an application. It then bounced around to our coordinator and psychologist and then Steve had to fill in some financial stuff. It seemed like a perfect solution, as I would receive a credit card to use for food, lodging, housing, etc. The only problem was that we got denied. Apparently, Steve makes too much money. I didn't really know this was an income-based thing until I found out that Steve would have to fill out a portion of the application. Nor did I have any idea of the maximum income level for the program. What I did know is that we were going to have to ask the Petersens for money. And asking people for money, even when you were giving them an organ, sucks.

Now, the Petersens have been all over it from the get-go, telling me they would take care of everything, and I knew they were totally willing to fly me out and take care of whatever expenses there might be. So, the difficulty with the money thing was my problem. Asking them just sucked. There has got to be a better way.

January 28, 2018

Here Comes the Sun - The Beatles

I am really looking forward to next month! My in-house visit to the University of Utah Medical Center is scheduled for Wednesday, February 14th.
Everyone has to visit the facility before they schedule the actual surgery. I get a CT scan of my kidneys, a chest scan, meet the docs who will be cutting me

open, take the tour, etc. And I get to meet Nurse Teresa!

Because my labs were suspect, the medical center wants me to come in for some over-the-top process that is guaranteed to put all doubt aside. I don't know the science behind it, but for kidneys, it's apparently the most accurate test. What I do know is that the magic number is 80. Anything below 80 is failing; above 80 and I'm most likely in like Flynn. That is what I am really anticipating. I want someone to finally give the green light and tell me that all systems are GO. I cannot do the Wednesday tour until they have positive results from this test. Yes, I'm sure the test involves sticking me with more needles. No, I do not know the name of the test. They told me, and I recorded it on my phone. I just can't remember because it's a difficult name. I want to say it sounds like Snuffleupagus.

I'm flying into Salt Lake City on a Thursday night to be there first thing Friday morning for the test. They should have the results Monday or Tuesday at the latest. If I pass, I will go ahead with Wednesday's planned activities. If I fail the test—and let's face it, I have failed two tests already, which is why I keep repeating lab work and why I am doing this one last test—it's all over. I don't want to think about failing. Truthfully, I'm pretty sure the donation is going to happen. I don't know why I think that. I cannot explain it. But I think I was meant to do this. So, positive thoughts all around!

I am also looking forward to meeting the Petersens. They offered to fly me back home in between my two hospital visits, as there is a pretty good gap. However, as I explained to them, I have a big presentation coming up and can do more to prepare for it in Utah than at home.

Leaving on a Jet Plane - Peter Paul and Mary

This afternoon, I flew to Salt Lake City, picked up a rental, and drove to Ozz's house. This is the first trip to the medical center where it all happens, and it makes everything a little more real. I knew it would. Like everything before, I have been proactive in getting this done. I scheduled this trip as soon as I could and I looked forward to it as one of those moments when I would feel a little more anticipation, a little more, "whoa, am I really doing this?"

The second trip will be the actual surgery. I don't know when that will be. I told the Petersens, my job is to get all the prelim stuff done: pass the labs, pass the exams, do the screenings and physicals, and be ready to go physically, mentally, and financially. Essentially, I need to get the green light from the medical center. Then, it is in their court.

I do wish this trip was less stressful. My day at the medical center is next Wednesday and that day won't even happen unless I pass my labs tomorrow. I'm confident we'll crush it though. Let's do this thing!

71

February 9, 2018

Pressure - Billy Joel

Got up early this morning and took care of my usual morning business, completely emptying everything in my bowels and bladder. I was instructed to fast the night before for my test, which I did. I drove to the University of Utah Medical Center. I was really looking forward to meeting the fabulous Nurse Teresa. She had been there from the beginning–calling to tell me I was next in line; telling me every time I passed or failed a test; educating me on everything kidney; and answering all my questions, even the stupid ones. I felt like I already knew her.

When Teresa and I met in person, it was just like I thought it would be. She was as kind and personal as she was over the phone. After we chatted a bit, she took me to a room and introduced me to Nurse Patience, who would be administering the iothalamate (io-thala-mate) test. (It took me about a week to be able to pronounce that correctly.) The iothalamate test measures the GFR and was described to me as "the gold standard of kidney exams." This is the test to end all kidney tests and will definitely determine my eligibility to donate an organ. As serious as this test was, it was pure comedy taking the exam. I wish I had it on camera. After Teresa left, the first thing Nurse Patience did was take my blood. Then she walked me to the bathroom, handed me a cup and told me to fill it up. Hmm. I said, "I don't think there's anything in the tank. I peed earlier and you guys told me to fast, so this may be a little difficult." She shut the door, but I could hear her on the other side of the door. As if I was not under enough pressure already.

What do you know? It worked! After I triumphantly completed the assignment, I opened the door and sure enough, there stood Nurse Patience, ready to collect my sample and walk me back to the room. Next thing on the list was to inject something into one of my triceps. Yay! Then Nurse Patience gave me three small cups of water. When I say small, we're talking about the little paper cone cups at the water cooler. She then walked out and said she would be back in an hour to repeat the process. She must think I have a very small bladder.

When she returned an hour later, she took my blood and then walked me to the bathroom again with the same expectation as before. I said, "Wait a minute here. I do not think the test is considering that we are at 5,000 feet in elevation and the air is bone dry. I haven't had a drop of moisture since yesterday, other than the three shots of water you gave me an hour ago. This dry air is sucking those little drops of water right out of my skin. It is not going to my bladder. There is nothing there." She was cool and listened to my argument, but procedures are procedures, and this test was to be exact. I summoned all the moisture in my body and directed it to my bladder and--yes!--I miraculously peed again, with Nurse Patience waiting just outside.

We walked back to our room where she gave me another drop of water. Not three as before—one! One little, tiny cone cup. We're talking one and a half swallows of water. I pleaded for more, but my cries fell upon deaf ears. Nurse Patience had no give. Then I waited forty-five minutes for her to come back and repeat the process. First, she took my blood and then we walked the walk of terror down the hall to the bathroom. It felt like that Twilight Zone scene when the hall grows longer and longer.

This time, Patience started giving me a little encouragement. It was hard to believe I was having this conversation with an adult. I felt like I was being potty-trained. "Come on, this is the last round. You can produce something! Just get it to this little mark." She showed me the level on the specimen cup that I had to meet for the test to be valid. I realized that if I didn't hit that mark then the entire morning and this test was shot. When we arrived at the bathroom, I said to Nurse Patience, "look, we're a team right? We have been together for three hours now trying to get this test completed. Could you be a team player and take a walk down the hall while I'm in here? Peeing with an audience, even though you're on the other side of the door, adds to the pressure. And right now, I don't need any more pressure." She was sweet and did what I asked.

When I completed the final draining, I exited the bathroom and raised the cup in victory. I gave a triumphant "woot! woot!" and the nurses' station came to life. Nurse Patience took the sample and shipped it and all the other blood and urine from the last three plus hours to the Mayo Clinic. I was surprised to hear they did not do the lab work in house. I asked Nurse Patience why I couldn't have done the test at home if they were just going to ship it to the Mayo Clinic. She said that was a good question. And that was that.

February 9, 2018: Evening

Come Together - The Beatles

I am staying at Ozz's house and there is nobody here.
It's kinda nice because I am working on a keynote for
a special needs conference in San Antonio next
Saturday called The Tapestry Conference. I was
working away and had this thought that this whole
process was happening, and I had never
communicated directly to Jenny. We had not emailed
each other directly, no texts, no nothing. All my
contact had been with Steve. I put my laptop down. I
needed to meet Jenny. And their house was not far
from Ozz's. So, I texted Steve.

I said, "Hey, the Olympics are on. I'm going to go to
fro-yo and then I'm going to watch the Olympics. You
guys want to go get a fro-yo?" They were in, so I
drove over to pick them up. I was a little nervous
driving over there. I had gone through this process,
been stuck with a needle too many times to count, put
the pressure on labs to expedite results, and had
been aggressive with everything in this process to
help out this woman, and I did not know Jenny from
Eve.

I was not sure what to open with. "Hi, I'm Rick, your
kidney donor?" How about, "Hello. I was in the
neighborhood and thought I'd drop off a kidney?" Or "I
got a call that someone here needed a kidney?" I
decided not to diffuse my anxiety with a corny remark.
Wait, what about, "Hi. I'm Rick, do you know why I am
able to donate a kidney? Because I am very
organ-ized." Ha! That's a keeper.

I arrived at the Petersens' and texted that I was there. Hey, nobody knocks anymore. Right? Steve came out of the house first and we fist bumped. When Jenny came out, I really did not know what to do. Should I give her a hug? I'm thinking, I'm giving her a kidney, so this is probably a hug moment. I gave her a hug and asked if things were going to be awkward between us. She said no. So, good icebreaker. We jumped in the car and went to the local fro-yo.

The three of us talked for hours about everything. Super, super good to just sit down with them and talk and get to know them face-to-face. Jenny's one kidney is functioning at 11%. She feels like there is a clock ticking on her life. I suppose she has every reason to feel that way. Her kidney is dying a little bit every day. Can you even imagine that? Can you see the wicked witch turning the hourglass over and telling you, "This is how long you have to live"?

I knew so little about this family and was intrigued by everything. I asked Steve and Jenny about Jenny's declining kidney. This is Jenny's story.

Ultra-Abbreviated Kidney Story of Jenny Petersen, as told by me (and probably not completely accurate)

When Steve and Jenny had their first child, they both got life insurance policies; Jenny's policy was quite small. Fast forward thirteen years, to 2015, and Jenny started feeling strongly that she should increase her policy. She kept getting this distinct, persistent feeling. She said it felt spiritual. So, Steve and Jenny decided to call the insurance company, and the company sent someone to the Petersens' house to do bloodwork on Jenny.

A couple weeks later, they got a letter from the insurance company, saying they would increase the policy, but at a much higher rate because Jenny's creatinine levels were elevated. Jenny asked what could cause that elevation and the insurance person said it could mean issues with her kidneys or possible dehydration. Jenny was sure it was dehydration. She went to a lab shortly after that and her numbers were still elevated. At that point, the insurance company suggested that she see a nephrologist.

Steve found a nephrologist who said Jenny needed to do lab work once more before she would see her. The labs showed that her levels were even more elevated than before. When she saw the nephrologist, the doctor ran additional tests, did an ultrasound, and discovered that Jenny had only one functioning kidney. The doctor told Jenny that elevated creatinine was normal in someone with a solitary kidney, and that Jenny should not worry. She told Jenny to repeat the labs in six months and to come back and see her in a year.

When Jenny did her lab work six months later, her creatinine levels were worsening, and the nephrologist asked her to come in. It was at that appointment that she learned she would need a transplant. This was April 2016.

Jenny couldn't officially start looking for a donor until she was approved for a transplant; one of the criteria was that her kidney function had to drop below 20%. She was approved on June 7, 2017, and Steve sent out his letter on June 10, 2017, asking for donors. The transplant center generated a list of potential donor candidates based on those who replied to the letter, and the testing began. The Petersens had both of their families, along with friends, neighbors, and everybody who replied to the letter, tested. Nobody was a match! And you know the rest of the story...

It was a fantastic evening with the Petersens. We joked, laughed, and got to know each other. So cool to hear their story and to get to know them. Such great people. I simply shake my head at what Jenny, Steve, and the whole family have been going through. It's just amazing to me.

Of course, we also talked about my donation journey so far, all the ups and downs of testing, and the iothalamate results that were coming. It's all riding on those results and we know it.

February 12, 2018

I Wanna be a Cowboy - Boys Don't Cry

Today is Monday and I'm still in Utah. I spent the weekend with friends and family and got a lot of work done. It is amazing how much work I can get done when I am alone.

Probably the highlight was when I went to an assisted living facility and kidnapped my great uncle, Beech Adams. I took the old cowboy to his farm where I have fantastic memories from my childhood. It was super cool spending time with him and hearing the old stories, which never get old for me. Beech is a legend, and he won't be around much longer.

My thoughts have continually been on the iothalamate test. It is the very reason I am here. EVERYTHING is riding on that test. I am hoping to get positive results today.

February 12, 2018: Evening

Tomorrow - Annie

I checked in at my good friend, Shaun Miner's, house today. I'll be staying here until I fly home on Wednesday. After I got settled, I called the transplant department, hoping that the results of my iothalamate test were in. They were not.

I am pretty anxious. Whatever I am feeling, I multiply that by 10 to try to understand how the Petersens are feeling. They know exactly what is going on here and what is riding on this iothalamate test. (I am getting way better at pronouncing that, by the way.) I shot Steve a text saying, "No results today. Tomorrow is the day we celebrate. I'll let you know as soon as I hear anything."

February 13, 2018

Call Me - Blondie

This morning, I was feeling agitated. I could tell it was going to be a clock-watcher day. I also did not sleep well last night. I needed the results of that iothalamate to put my mind at ease. I guess I am more of a worrier than I thought. The results have to come today. Tomorrow is my day at the transplant center. What the heck is taking them so long?

Around mid-day, my cell rang, and I could see it was the transplant center. I answered and Nurse Teresa sounded in good spirits. She said, "We received the results from your iothalamate. You're at 90%, which is good! So, everything's good and we'll see you tomorrow." I busted in with a couple hoots and sighs of relief, followed by thank yous. We discussed my coming in tomorrow at 9 AM. The whole day was planned out. I get to meet the surgeons. Then we are going to do the CT scan and look at my kidneys. Then the chest X-ray, and much, much more!

I felt like I had won the lottery, and I could not wait to get off the phone with Teresa to call Steve, which is what I did 1.2 seconds later. When Steve answered his cell, there was no hello. I could only hear sounds of a meeting in progress and some shuffling, as Steve made his exit to speak to me.

Steve: Ricky D

Me: I totally nailed that test.

Steve: You passed?

Me: I passed. A solid 90%. Come on man, was there any doubt?

Steve: So glad.

We talked only briefly as he needed to call Jenny. I could hear the elation in his voice. What a sweet feeling this was. I love it! I love it! It's done! It's over. The rest is just a formality. I am meant to do this. I could not help but get emotional and I called and told Robin.

Robin: Oh, my gosh.

Me: I know.

Robin: How do you feel?

Me: Spiritual. You know when I went looking for a book to read about giving a kidney and all the books had spirituality written all over them? I am beginning to understand that it is a spiritual process. I don't know if you can be a living donor and not feel the spirit.

Robin: You know it's not going to feel good when it happens right?

Me: Yes, but you know, it's giving someone life. How can you not feel good about that? I know I'm going to feel like garbage. I know these things. It's just. I just felt so good about it so many times. I'm ready to go.

I am totally stoked about the kidney test! Totally! There is only one thing left to do, and that is to look at the kidney through a CT scan, do the chest scan, and have the in-house visit. The board will approve me next week and then it will be in the Petersens' hands. EVERYTHING IS GOING ACCORDING TO PLAN!

February 13, 2018: Evening

What's Going On - Marvin Gaye

At 3:30 this afternoon, I went to the Ogden Temple with Shaun and his wife, Rachel. As always, I turned off my cell when I went in. It is a beautiful temple, and we had a really good experience. Afterwards, I told Shaun and Rachel that we needed to celebrate my passing my labs with flying colors. My treat, let's eat. So, we went to a Hawaiian barbecue place not far away. As we were enjoying our meal, I turned my cell on.

After my cell booted up, I saw a notification that Nurse Teresa had called three times. She had also left a voicemail at 3:47 PM. Without delay, I hit play and listened to her voicemail. She said, "Hi, Rick. This is Teresa at the transplant center. I just need to talk to you when you get a moment. It's just about your lab results. If you can call me as soon as you can."

The tone of her voice was not good, and I felt a dark wave come over me. I called her back immediately, but it went straight to her voice mail. I left a message. I have two other numbers for the transplant center, and I called them as well. Nobody home. Nothing but crickets. I left more voicemails, explaining that Teresa had left me a message and would someone please call me back. I tried not to sound concerned, but I am sure I did not pull that off.

I played Teresa's message for Shaun and Rachel. I said, "her tone suggests that there's a problem." Shaun and Rachel were supportive and offered a few suggestions, like "maybe it's nothing" or "it's something simple, Let's not worry about it." I listened to the message again and again. I said to no one, "What? What about my lab results do we need to discuss? I passed! I passed with flying colors!" I cannot go for the remainder of the day without knowing what it is that we need to discuss. But nobody at the transplant center was talking. I called Nurse Teresa's number again and again because there was a pit in my stomach.

I tried to be positive, but something was wrong. NO WAY WAS I GOING TO TELL THE PETERSENS. No sense in having them toss and turn all night. After we got home, I called Robin. She predictably kept it positive, saying: "You don't know... You could be jumping to conclusions... No point in worrying about it... You'll find out tomorrow." The Winter Olympics were on, so I watched Shaun White win the snowboard halfpipe gold medal and I went to bed.

Only, I could not get to sleep, so I got up to do a little work. I reread the next day's itinerary over and over and tried to get myself to chill.

February 14, 2018

Don't You Want Me - The Human League

I did not sleep well again last night. I woke up several times. At 3:00 AM, I was up for the day. That's 2:00 AM on my California internal clock. I checked in first thing this morning for my scheduled appointment, ready to go about the day as planned.

A nurse I did not know took my weight at 195 lbs. And height at a hair under 6'1. Not only am I growing wider, but I'm shrinking. Gotta get on that. The nurse asked me to follow her to the examination room. As we walked down the hall, we passed by the nurses' station. There were half a dozen nurses and one doctor there, all engaged in conversation. When I approached, two nurses looked up at me and then turned back to the rest of them. All conversation ceased.

Could it be more obvious? I'm sure they're not talking about me! Right? I almost stopped and asked, "Hey everyone, good morning! What's the good word today? What are we talking about? Come on, out with it!" But I held my tongue.

The nurse took me to my room and told me that Teresa would be in shortly. When Teresa came in, she was smiling, but I knew it was a cover. She shook my hand and started the small talk. I told her, "Just tell me the bad news." She said, "Okay. They made an error at the Mayo Clinic. A clinical error. And you are not at 90 milliliters per minute filtration. You are at 75, and 80 is our cutoff. So, you don't reach the cut off."

When she said that, I was devastated. Even though I knew—I mean—I kind of knew it was coming. Right? But this is lame. Lame! I was kind of prepared for it, right? I just thought, "I'm going to be positive about this." I'm praying the whole time for spirit and strength. Praying mostly for Jenny and Steve and their family. Just worried for them.

But how could this happen? I asked Teresa. A clinical error? How is that possible? She said that the data was entered manually, and someone made a mistake and entered 90 when it was actually 75.

Me: What? The Mayo Clinic? The Mayo Clinic enters these things manually and they accidentally wrote down 90 instead of 75?

Teresa: Yes

Me: Well, let's take it again!

Teresa: It won't make any difference.

Me: How do you know?

Teresa: This is a very accurate test and the Mayo Clinic...

Me: [interrupting] The Mayo Clinic just made a mistake. A huge mistake.

Teresa: Yes, but they fixed it. They went over the data, and you got a 75. For sure a 75. If you take it again, you'll get a 75. I'm sorry.

At this point, my brain was spinning. I had some tests in the gray area and probably failed some labs, although "failed" was never uttered. This was the very reason why we took this highly sensitive and accurate test. And now, I have officially been dismissed. It's over. I should call it a day, pack up and go. The only problem was there was not even an ounce of me that was saying, "well, you gave it your best. Let's move on." Heck NO! Nurse Teresa knew it too.

Me: Look. Let's talk about this.

Teresa: Okay.

Me: This stinks. Like this does not pass the smell test. And it's not even close. I'm just not buying it. There's been all these errors. Right. Like all these things that we just don't know about. So, let's take it again! I just happen to be fasting for the CT scan so I'm ready!

Teresa: I anticipated you would say that. There are two nurses who are trained and can give the iothalamate test. Neither are scheduled for today but we can call to see if either will come in.

Me: Well, let's make some calls!

Teresa: Our chances are still slim, even if we can get one of those nurses to come in.

Me: Why?

Nurse Teresa: Because you got 75 and the test is expensive. I need to get approval to repeat the test and that will be difficult.

Me: You mean the Mayo Clinic is going to charge us? This is America! If I go to a restaurant and they screw up my order, they fix it! If I order anything from anyone, they fix it! Mayo owes us a freebie! Look, call Mayo and let me talk to them. I have been here, away from my family and my work since Thursday night. They are not going to screw up the order and not give us a freebie!

Teresa: I'll make some calls.

Me: Look, Teresa. I don't mean to be a jerk about this. I like you and I have come a long way with this whole process. I am emotional about this because it's not about me. It's about a family who needs something that I am willing to give. And I'm pretty darn sure I am supposed to give it. You need to understand that I am going to fight for it. If I lose, I'm going down swinging. Will you help me fight for this?

Teresa: Yes

I can tell she's on board 100%. She's trying to be professional, but I know she's feeling it. I can see it in her eyes. They are full of compassion and determination. I can literally feel it. She's going to bat for us, and she won't stop swinging until she's out. I told her that I wanted to turn over every stone and do everything we could. She agreed.

Teresa left the room and all I could think about was that this was going to take a miracle. But my heart was pumping, and I felt like fighting someone. Preferably someone at the Mayo Clinic. LET'S GO! I'm so ready to throw down!

February 14, 2018: Still morning

Hungry Like a Wolf - Duran Duran

Luckily, I've got my phone with me to record this day as it happens. After Teresa left, I was left to my thoughts and emotions. I figured I would calm down in a few minutes, but I did not. I'm still pumped, and I don't show any signs of slowing down. Do I need to call the Petersens? I mean, I know I do, but at what point? I need to have something positive. Anything.

87

Nurse Teresa came in not long after she left. We got approved to repeat the test! BAM! Only problem is that one nurse cannot come in and the other nurse is trying to see if she can rearrange her schedule. I was like, COME ON PEOPLE! Let's make this happen!

I asked Teresa how we should proceed. I had all these meetings lined up and I'm sure the doctors don't want to meet with someone who failed the iothalamate test. She said we would go ahead with the day as planned. Then someone else came in with a bunch of paperwork to sign.

I flew through the paperwork. It was funny because there were places I signed that said I could walk away up until two weeks prior to the surgery. Yeah, I'm pretty sure I can walk away until they knock me out. I mean, what are they going to do? Stop me and throw me on the table? Hey buddy, you signed all the waivers and voted to move on with the process! Now hold still while we knock you out and cut into your gut.

They took my picture and entered all my info into the system. There were more questions and forms and yes, yes, yes, I know what I'm gettin' into! Then someone came in and did an EKG, so they got my heart rhythm. Then another woman came in to do blood work and more blood work. Because, you know, I can't get enough of that. By the way, this is not blood work related to the iothalamate. For all I know, it could be that the nurses just need practice sticking people. So, they send them to me because I'll never know the difference. I'm happy someone is sticking me, anyway. It shows progress and my heart is pounding, so I fill those vials at record speed.

I still have not calmed down since my conversation with Nurse Teresa. I am that guy who, if someone tells me I can't do something, I do it. But I don't want that to be the reason why I donate a kidney. It can't be. I should not want to donate just because someone tells me I can't. You know what I'm saying? So, anyway, I just kept thinking about it and my motivation and the logical and spiritual experiences that I've had about this. I questioned and thought about all of this and then I decided I was going to fight.

At this point, I'm having mixed feelings about the Transplant Center. I'm fighting for this, and they are pushing back. They tried to get me to walk out of here this morning and I'm telling them, I'm staying until we have explored every avenue. But here's the thing. I know we are on the same side. I know they are looking out for my health. I feel like I know my body, but they are the experts. I don't want to be sick down the road. I don't want to have to go through what Jenny Petersen is going through. What is the point of making one person healthy by making another person sick? Right? I totally and completely get that. It's all about my potential to develop kidney disease of any kind. I don't want that, the Transplant Center doesn't want that, and the Petersens definitely don't want that.

Teresa came in to say something and as she was leaving, I asked if I could talk to her alone for a minute. The nurse doing the blood work asked if she should leave. I told her yes, please, and that it would only be a minute and she left. So, it was just me and Teresa and I was worried I was going to...well I don't know? I was having a difficult time keeping my emotions in check and I was not sure what was going to happen.

I stood up and I could feel the spirit in my bones; however, I didn't cry. It was more of a strong, confident, fire-like sensation. I looked Teresa in the eyes and said, "I guess I'm getting a little emotional about this. I am not going to fight for this because everyone is telling me I can't do it. I am going to fight for this because I feel like it is the right thing to do. I feel like this is my job and that I am supposed to do this. I realize that nothing will be determined based on my feelings. I just want you to know that I am going to fight for this. At some point, I'm going to ask you to present my case to the board. And I know that you're not allowed to do that because my test was below an 80. But we're going to do this. I don't know how, but it's going to happen." We never broke eye contact and she said, "Okay." I could tell she meant it. I felt and knew she was going to do everything she could. It was a huge boost just knowing that.

The nurse came back in to finish the bloodletting and we were back to the flow. Another official looking person came in to really make sure I understood what I was getting into. She had all the paperwork they had sent me from the beginning, and we went over all of it. Then she said, "If you get to the point of surgery, you'll be in here for two to three days." I said, "What do you mean 'if'? It's a done deal."

Nurse Teresa entered again to tell me that Nurse Patience was coming in to repeat the iothalamate test! YES! Nurse Patience! I love it! Nurse Teresa also reminded me not to get my hopes up, because this test was exact, and I'll get another 75. I was like, yeah, yeah, yeah, whatever, let's rock and roll.

Time was no longer on my side, of course. We were cutting it close. My flight left at 5:50 PM, the iothalamate test was nearly four hours long, and Nurse Patience couldn't get there until after lunch time. So, fun times seeing if I can make my flight.

February 14, 2018: Mid-morning

Doctor! Doctor! - Thompson Twins

Next into my room was Doctor Harvest. He introduced himself and said he would be the surgeon who would collect my kidney. I asked him if he was okay speaking with me even though I had failed the iothalamate test. He was cool and said he was going to treat this visit with me the same as he would with anyone else going under the knife. The conversation shifted to the technical aspects of extracting my kidney. That was killer. He talked about how they enter from the front and unstick everything to get to the kidney. Totally killer.

We talked about follow-up visits and labs. I could do all of them at home in San Diego, with the exception of the one-year post donation clinic. They wanted me in Utah for that one. Doc was cool and asked if I had any questions. Truthfully, I did not pay full attention to everything he said because all I could think about was, "This guy is going to stick his hand through my belly and wiggle down around and through all my guts until he finds my kidney. Then, after cutting all the connectors in and out, grab it with his hand and pull it out. I mean, who doesn't want this guy's job?!"

Nurse Teresa came in just as Dr. Harvest was leaving. She was orchestrating this revolving door of everybody in and out. She said we might not get the CT scan of my kidney today because of the iothalamate test. But I could do the CT at my home lab. She then told me that a nephrologist named Doctor Brightside wanted to talk to me.

Next up was a walk to the radiology department for a chest X-ray. That was fun. Now I know what it's like to get a mammogram. Well, sort of. Okay, not really. I had to call the Petersens and I was just dreading it. I walked out of the radiology waiting room and called. I didn't get anything. No answer. So, I called Robin, and there we go, verbal diarrhea all over the place. I just had to let it out. It was therapeutic talking to her. She said, "this is insane!" I told her we were full steam ahead. We're going about this as if I got a 90 on my test. Then I noticed that Steve Petersen sent me a text. It was time to break the news.

I called Steve and I was pretty emotional. I said, "Look, I don't know how to tell you this…" I was pausing to search for the right words. He was just silent, like awkward silent. I said, "Look, first, I just want you to know that I'm here. I'm going through with everything at the hospital as planned. But the Mayo Clinic called, and they made a clerical error on my iothalamate test. I did not pass it."

I told Steve the 90% was not correct. Somebody blew it and recorded the wrong numbers. I actually got 75%. As you know, 80% is the cut off. He just said, "Man, this is a roller coaster." I told him I was fighting for this and that I demanded the Mayo Clinic give us a freebie. I said I was about to take the iothalamate test again. I told him, "I'm just sick about this whole thing and I apologize that things don't look so good." Steve said, "You got nothing to apologize for. You have gone the whole way. You've been willing to do this and you've done it."

We had planned to meet at the end of the day at our favorite restaurant, the Red Iguana. I said "no can do" because I had to take the iothalamate test again and I was risking missing my flight. So anyway, I had a really good conversation with Steve. It was emotional, but we ended on a good note.

February 14, 2018: Lunchtime

Mr. Brightside - The Killers

I walked back to my exam room, where Nurse Teresa was continuing the parade of health care workers, and she introduced me to Doctor Brightside. After we were introduced, Brightside asked jokingly if I had seen enough people today. I said something about how popular I was. He said, "Oh yeah, everybody here knows what's going on. This has never happened before, and it's got everyone scratching their heads. It's the talk of the town. This poor guy was told 90% and then later they said, 'psych, only 75!'" And yet, here I am. We're going forth.

Dr. Brightside is all about the numbers. He's a stats guy and so am I. So, right off the bat, I've got a good feeling about this dude. He starts laying out the numbers. He even has this app with all the data. We go over all my past test results, my body mass index, my 75% on the iothalamate, everything. He puts everything in and computes it. My chances of developing any kind of kidney disease down the road is 3.75%--not even 4%!

That's after I donate a kidney. Three point seventy five percent. Doc said, "Look, I'm your advocate. And if you want to fight this, we're on board and we will present this to the board." I replied, "But the board will not consider any case below 80%." He said, "Yep, you'll be the first."

I was going nuts about the board presentation. I was denied that opportunity first thing this morning and now I had a chance? I asked Dr. Brightside about the 80% number and where that came from. He explained that it's basically a random number that some kidney organization came up with and everyone went along with it! Are you kidney me!?

Brightside took me through the 80% and the reason behind it. There is logic to it, but at some point, they felt like they needed a number to cut potential donors off and they decided on 80. He explained, "We're gonna discuss this... We're discussing your case... We're going forward." He gave me more statistics and told me that this was a highly debatable topic. He said it was really hot and involved both conservative and liberal viewpoints.

I told Brightside that I would be taking the iothalamate test again and that we might not have this problem of submitting a 75%. All of this could go away with a better test result. He said, "Yeah, that's good, positive thinking, but you'll get a 75 again."

Talking with Dr. Brightside was the highlight of the day. He was really fun and highly motivating. This dude was my greatest advocate and he told me so. We discussed everything in relation to kidneys, giving a kidney, and living with one kidney. I told him how stoked I was and that I was ready to go. He said that I would not be allowed in the board presentation, so I asked if I could write a letter. He said that was a good idea.

Take a Chance on Me - Abba

Like clockwork, Nurse Teresa came in as Dr. Brightside was leaving. I don't know how she does that. She had been timing her entrances and exits perfectly all day. Was there a button in here that people pressed when they were leaving? As he was exiting, Dr. Brightside told Teresa, right here in this room, in front of me, that my case would be presented to the board next Thursday. She nodded in agreement. You could tell this had been something they had discussed behind the scenes earlier. Shoot, I'm sure there were all kinds of things going on behind the scenes today.

Teresa: I'll get the results from today plus everything we already have, and your case will be presented to our selection committee.

Me: Next Thursday? As in a week from tomorrow?

Teresa: Yes. We've come a long way today, haven't we?

Me: Yes, I can't believe the difference from this morning's doom and gloom until now.

Of course, I think it's all because of Dr. Brightside. I know he's back there telling everyone to pump the breaks and let's discuss this. I wish I could be a fly on the wall when the board meets just to see him laying out the facts like he did with me.

Teresa: I'll have everything ready to go.

Me: Wait! But you won't be there! You'll be on vacation, diving in the Caribbean.

Teresa: Nurse Downer can present you.

Me: I'm not sure how I feel about that. I want you to present my case. Maybe we should wait until I get the CT scan of my kidney, you are back, and everything will be in place.

Teresa: That's an option. Let's get everything done and discuss it later. Either way, we'll be ready.

Me: Would a letter from me help?

Teresa: It might. What we'll do is, we'll present your case and see what everybody says. Then we'll do your CT scan.

Me: So, the case will be presented before I get a CT scan?

Teresa: Yes. We'll talk about you, make sure everything is good, but it won't be the final presentation. This is a special circumstance and will take some time for decisions to be made. So, you go home and get your CT scan and I will get it to the board. But you won't be able to do it before next Thursday.

Me: Let me ask you about the board. Is it a majority rule or does everybody have to agree?

Teresa: Everyone has to agree. If there is one dissenting vote, then it won't happen. So, yeah, we want everyone to agree. We don't want to fail.

Me: How many people are on the board?

Teresa: I believe there are nine people.

Me: So, if only one person in nine says no?

Teresa: If one person says no, they're concerned for this reason or that reason…

Me: Oh my gosh! So, there's always a stick in the mud. Always one!

Teresa: So, yeah, you do that letter, and we'll do our best to present your case.

Me: When my next iothalamate test results come back, you won't have to worry about this presentation. I won't need a letter. We'll get that CT scan and done deal.

Teresa: OK. OK. Sounds good. All right. What questions do you have for me?

Me: Do you feel good about presenting my case?

Teresa: Yeah. You've talked to a lot of people today. I know that they've been very thorough with you. Any questions?

Me: I'm good. Thank you.

Nurse Teresa: You're welcome. And if everything goes through, when do you want to look at donating?

Me: I've actually talked to the Petersens about it. I told them I would be ready to go when they are. Jenny wants to aim for the fall. Last I heard, she was looking at September. October and November are also on the table.

Teresa: Okay, we don't have anything on the books for that time. But just know that if it has been a year since your initial labs, we will need to do those over. If I remember correctly, your first labs were in December. I can double check. Yes. And that way we just have to look at everything. Make sure that nothing's changed.

Me: It will be done before winter. I can't handle any more holes in my arms.

Teresa: You'll have to. Because they put an I.V. in your arm for the surgery.

Me: Yeah, that'll be the last one. Oh, one last thing. If for any reason it doesn't go through, do we have backup? Have other people come forward for Jenny? Anyone you know who is compatible?

Teresa: I would move forward with the next person. You were just a better match than the other ones.

Me: So back to square one with the next person up? They would go through the same things that I just went through, starting with the blood and tissue match?

Teresa: Yes. Are you thinking we should start moving forward with someone else?

Me: No, I feel good about this. However, there is a life at stake here, so we need to look at everything. If my next iothalamate test comes back and it's not good, then we'll reevaluate. But I'm fine. I mean, I'm fine at 75. To be honest with you. I feel good about it. Even if it comes back with 75. I'm good. If it comes back at 90, I'm really good. Yeah, 90, then we're great.

Teresa: We'll just move forward with everything that comes back in. If it's 75, we'll have another discussion with Dr. Brightside and discuss with the team. OK?

Me: All right. Dr. Brightside told me they've never accepted anyone lower than 80. Correct?

Teresa: No one has ever been submitted to the board lower than an 80.

Me: First time for everything.

Teresa: That's why it would have to be a big discussion. That's our requirement.

Me: I get it. Teresa, thank you for everything.

Teresa: You're welcome.

February 14, 2018: Afternoon

Here We Go Again – Whitesnake

Nurse Patience was in the room before my conversation ended with Teresa. She was prepping away and pumped to come in on her off day to do another iothalamate test with me. Yeah, not really. Actually, she seemed fine with it. Nurse Patience is pretty cool.

We began the exam and did the same thing we did Friday. She took blood, I peed, and then I looked for my swig of water.

Nurse Patience: We're going to do a bladder analysis before you drink.

Me: Well, we didn't do that last time! I don't even know what that is.

Nurse Patience: We're going to do an ultrasound of your bladder and see if there is anything in there.

Me: Are you going to squirt jelly on my belly like when my wife was pregnant?

Nurse Patience: Yes. If there is something in there, we'll catheterize you to drain the rest out.

Me: I'm sorry, WHAT DID YOU SAY!?!?!? You're going to stick a catheter in, in, in, ME? Are you freaking kidding me? What a sweet Valentine's Day treat for me. Good grief.

So now I'm sweating bullets! She puts this jelly on my belly and busts out the ultrasound. Flash back to my five kids and all the ultrasounds my wife had. We got the same thing going on here and she's looking at my bladder to see if it's completely empty. You cannot imagine the pleading in my heart to almighty God, OH PLEASE BE EMPTY! PLEASE!!!!!!!

Nurse Patience: Nope, nothing in there. You are empty.

Me: Thank the Lord!

She gave me my swig of water and left.

This is interesting. This entire day, I have been making journal entries through my cell. When Nurse Patience leaves the room and tells me she'll be back in an hour or 45 minutes, I whip out my phone and start journaling the day.

So, the test is the exact same except Nurse Patience is going to check my bladder every time I pee. She lets me pee in the exam room instead of walking the hall of terror. I think she's messing with my mind though. When she shuts the door, I can hear footsteps, as if she is walking away. When in fact, I think it is all a facade and she is right behind the door, walking in place.

So next time I peed, I dug deeper than any man ever dug before. The pressure was at an all-time-high! No way they're sticking a catheter in me! Must empty bladder completely! Keep in mind that it is now afternoon and I have been fasting since yesterday. Plus, remember that Utah is the driest place on earth. Everyone who lives here has multiple lip moisturizers in every possible accessible container. Oh, plus the altitude. So, it was not any easier putting pee into the cup, second time around.

Every time I urinated, Nurse Patience did the bladder ultrasound. And every time, I was pleading for the powers of heaven to shine on my bladder. The last round was intense. Remember, I needed to reach the line on the specimen cup or the entire test, and the day would be invalid. As with the first test, I summoned every ounce of fluid in my body to head to my bladder and I passed. I passed, I passed! I freakin' passed!

When we finished, Nurse Patience was all over me about downing serious fluids. She said that going on an airplane without any fluids could set me up for possible blood clots. What? Yeah. Well, apparently, dehydration plus sitting plus elevation equals increased risk of clots. So, from the second we completed the iothalamate, I was lapping up water like a parched dog from a garden hose.

I ran down to the cafeteria where I cashed in a little gift card the nurses had given me. Then I ran to my rental car and jammed to the airport. I'm sleeping in my own bed tonight. What an unreal day. Happy Valentine's Day!

February 19, 2018

I Want to Fly Away - Lenny Kravitz

Been super busy. I flew home from Salt Lake City last Wednesday night. No blood clots. No missed flights. No problems. It's all good. Thursday was my one day at home. Friday, I flew to San Antonio. Saturday, I gave a keynote presentation, plus two breakout sessions and a final wrap up at a special needs conference for parents. It might have been the most rewarding experience of my professional career. I just love speaking to parents in smaller conferences. It's easier to connect with them and to teach and learn. It's because these people are what I am, a parent doing his best with what he's got.

Sunday, I flew to Las Vegas, where I met up with my family. We then drove the rest of the way to my sister Katherine's house in St. George, Utah. This was the start of our much anticipated, big family ski vacation! Monday, we were supposed to go to my friend's cabin, which was close to the resort. However, it dumped snow all day. Because the weather was bad, we decided not to drive up the mountain and, instead, hunkered down at Uncle Bryan and Aunt Jenny's house in Cedar City.

Now, you would think that my mind would be on getting the test results for my second iothalamate test, but it wasn't. I mean, I was thinking about it, but I wasn't worried. I knew they had the results. And I know I passed.

I would bet anything the transplant center got the results the Thursday after I took the test, Friday at the latest. This is pure speculation, of course, but let's go with it. So, if the transplant center received the results on Friday, then why haven't they called to tell me? Answer, because I passed. I passed and nobody knows what to make of it. The University of Utah doctors are calling the Mayo Clinic, asking how did this guy get a 75% on the iothalamate test on a Friday and above an 80% on Wednesday?

Can't you just see it? This is the gold standard for kidney tests. It is absolute, right? All those doctors and nurses who were like, yeah Rick, this is really admirable of you to take this test again, but it'll be 75 again. Don't expect anything different. Now all these chemists and kidney nerds are getting together in the nerdery, scratching their heads, trying to figure out what the heck happened? Dr. Brightside is no doubt probing the hardest, making calls to his fellow nephrologists, saying, "check this out. We got a potential donor who got a 75 and we dismissed him. But he would not go home and insisted on taking the exam again. So, he takes it again a few days later and passes!" What's the protocol on this? Answer: nobody knows because it's never happened before.

So, they all take the weekend to process and maybe test some more and try to come up with answers.

February 20, 2018

Don't Bring Me Down - Electric Light Orchestra

Today is Tuesday, our first day of skiing at Brian Head. About halfway through the day, I got a voicemail notice from the Transplant Center. It was a call from Nurse Downer, who is subbing for Nurse Teresa while she is on vacation. I called Downer back right there on the slopes. No more delay. I could not wait to hear what she had to say.

Nurse Downer: Hey, so your results are in. You know...they're not so good.

Me: Oh (thinking I got like a 70 or something now. Rapid depression setting in)

Nurse Downer: (downer voice) You got an 83.

Me: (upper voice) That's passing!

Nurse Downer: Yeah. But nobody knows what to make of this.

As our conversation continued, all I could think about was, this woman has been coached on what to say. I could just see her higher-ups telling her, look, we don't want this guy getting too excited in case we decide to rip the carpet out from under him. I kept saying, "I passed!" and she kept saying, "yes, but...doctors need to get together and talk about it....figure this out." I really wanted to say, "The doctors HAVE been talking about it. You think I don't know the results have been in for a few days?" But I kept it to myself. The basic theme of our short conversation was, how can you be a 75 one day and an 83 a few days later? And that's where we're at.

I am sure that they're reeling at the U and the Mayo Clinic. And who knows where they're talking about this. First, they told me I got a 90%. Then that turned out to be a clerical error and it was really a 75. At least four medical professionals at the Transplant Center said the 75 would not change if I retook the test, and two of those people were kidney doctors. They were all very professional that day, but I could sense some attitude like, why are we doing this? It's going to be the same result. This is a waste of time, money, and personnel. But it didn't stay the same. Just a few days later, it changed to a passing grade of 83! Which–hello!--is closer to a 90 than to a 75!

I jumped on a lift and went to find my family on the slopes. I should have been pumped, but Nurse Downer stifled my stoke. Nevertheless, I still had the satisfaction of passing the dreaded iothalamate test and I was still very much in the game.

I called Steve Petersen because I was pretty sure they were waiting to hear the news. I relayed all the information, from the 83 passing score to Nurse Downer downplaying the grade to my thoughts on everything. Bottom line, we were down but not out, back in but not through the roof.

February 21, 2018

No More Words - Berlin

So, as far as the Petersens go...not really sure how to say this. At the very beginning, we established an open communication. Their position has always been for me to share whatever information I feel comfortable sharing. They have never put the slightest pressure on me to share or not share and they have always been respectful. And by "they," I mean Steve, since he's the only one I communicate with.

The only problem is that my road to donation has been all over the map. Ever since I wrote my first book about being a dad of kids with special needs, my life has literally become an open book. I generally feel comfortable sharing everything, even though I typically tell myself to shut it. Here's my constant dilemma. I pass a lab, or interview, or scan, or test. I think this will really make the Petersens happy. I want to make people happy. It's what I do. Who doesn't want to be the bearer of good news? So, I share. Every time I pass something is one step closer to the operating table.

It's fun, like winning another game. The Petersens are my team and I'm a team player. What good is a win that I keep to myself? It's way more fun to celebrate with my team. So, I share the triumphs and we jump up and down on home plate, spike the ball, and bounce around.

The problem with that is, when we receive bad news that negates the good news, then I am the bearer of that bad news. And nobody wants to be the bearer of bad news. I hate bad news. And I especially hate delivering bad news right after the good. You see where I am coming from here? I'm saying it completely and totally sucked to tell Steve and Jenny I failed the iothalamate test. It was gut wrenching.

For me, I can live just fine with or without one of my kidneys. But this has never been about me. It's about Jenny. IT IS ABOUT LIFE. Sacred and precious LIFE. Think about that. When I relay bad news to the Petersens, life becomes threatened. The life of a wife and mother of four kids has already been compromised. Her life is on a steady downward spiral. That life extinguishes unless modern medicine and an organ donor prevail. That's where I am able to help. And when modern medicine tells me my organ is not qualified, my stomach churns. So, I tell myself to remain quiet until it's time to celebrate the championship. I should call them only when it's time to cut down the nets, but I just can't hold it in.

February 22, 2018

Land of Confusion - Genesis

Today is Thursday, the 22nd of February. I talked to Steve the other day after I got the results of my iothalamate test, even though I said I was done giving the Petersens information. But, as I said, I really felt like they were waiting to hear, and I just can't shut my big yapper!

I just got off the phone with Nurse Downer a few minutes ago (Teresa is still on vacation). Downer told me they're still discussing and trying to figure out how this happened. But get this! She told me that now she has good news: "You scored an 83, which was highly unusual. So, they took the same sample and tested it twice. So, the test you took on Wednesday, they retested all of those samples twice at the Mayo Clinic. One was an 83 and one was a 90." Uh, WHAT?!

Ok, now, I'm a huge skeptic. All I can think is, "Why didn't this woman tell me before that I had a legit 90?" She only told me I had an 83.

Downer doesn't give me a time frame and I don't ask. Because now I have this pessimistic attitude and the way she is explaining everything makes me think they retested right after getting the first result, and they knew I got a 90 when I talked to them two days ago. I could be wrong, but I still think there is a lot of coaching and debate going on behind the scenes. Something isn't sitting right with me.

Nurse Downer: The Mayo Clinic and our nephrologists are going back and forth. They are trying to decipher how you can get a 90 and then have a clinical error bring you down to a 75. On your second test you got an 83 and then we wanted to make sure it was correct, so the sample was retested and it came out a 90.

Me: Wait, Nurse Downer, let me restate this just to make sure I'm on the same page because I'm a little thrown off by the second 90 score (I restate everything).

Nurse Downer: Correct.

Me: So, there are a total of four numbers now from these tests. There is only one number below the passing grade of 80. The ultimate question is, which number are you going with?

Nurse Downer: That's the good news. They are going to take your original score of 90.

Me: So, I'm approved?

Nurse Downer: Yes.

Me: (Elated but still skeptical) How can that possibly be? It was a clinical error, wasn't it?

Nurse Downer: Yes, well, it's a very highly technical equation.

Me: OK. Sweet. So, now I have one last thing to do, right? The scan?

Nurse Downer: Yes.

Just one thing left to do. Just one more test to pass. I have to get a scan of my kidneys to make sure I do have kidneys. A lot of people only have one kidney, and they simply don't know it. If you were born with one kidney, how would you ever know? So hopefully, I have two. They also need to look at them to see which one to take. I have been told they always leave the bigger one with the donor, and also that, most of the time, they harvest the left one.

Finally, I was cleared by the transplant team. I will do the CT in San Diego.

February 22, 2018: Evening

Carry On My Wayward Son - Kansas

I called Steve when I got off the phone with Nurse Downer and told him the whole iothalamate thing. Suffice it to say, he was like, "What? What?! This is nuts. This has just been a whirlwind of craziness." This seems to be a recurring theme of our conversations. I mean, we literally just had this same conversation but with different numbers. Just when we think things are going to make sense, they get weirder. But we're not complaining because when all is said and done, I got a 90! Doesn't really matter how I got there. I got a freakin' 90!

I told Steve of my internal struggle of whether to share or not share information, simply because this whole iothalamate test was such a gut wrencher. Steve and I understand each other and it's good to be communicating with a good dude through this circus. The Petersens know I am fighting for them and for this. They knew I was fighting to do it when I had a 75! We talked about how crazy this experience has been. We also discussed the last step, the CT scan. The way it's going, I'll probably fail that. Maybe I'll only have one kidney and then two days later, they'll say, "Oh wait, there it is!"

February 26, 2018

I'm Still Standing - Elton John

I've done my due diligence. I've listened, read, calculated, and dissected the science. I understand the risks. I found people who were unhappy and/or were in poor health following their kidney donation. They were hard to find, but they are out there. It doesn't sway me.

What I really enjoy is hearing from others who have donated. You'll recall my attempt to find a good book and I turned them all down. They just didn't resonate with me. Today, I got an email from my brother Mike, who forwarded an email from his friend, Gary. Gary donated a kidney to his brother, and his brother is a beast. Dude ran the Boston Marathon four months post-surgery in 3:15.

Now this is what I want to hear. People crushing it post-donation. Gary says he cannot tell he is without

111

a kidney. No physical effects at all. I wish I had access to more guys like Gary. I don't need the motivation to do this, but it's so rad to hear about donors killing it.

March 3, 2018

Takin' Care Of Business - Bachman–Turner Overdrive

Nurse Teresa is back from vacation, and I don't intend on letting her ease back into work. Even if it is a Saturday! She can share her vacation pics with the others later. Time is of the essence! Let's go people! We have one more thing to get done!

From: Rick Daynes
Sent: Saturday, March 3, 2018 6:12 AM
To: Nurse Teresa
Subject: CT?

Hi Teresa!

I trust you had the best vacation ever! Hey, just wanted to touch base. As I'm sure you know, I am a freak of nature and passed the Olith...blah blah test. Only thing I have left is the CT scan. Last I heard from Downer, she was coordinating something at Sharp here in San Diego. That was over a week ago. Any chance we can get that done?

Thanks,

Rick Daynes

March 12, 2018

Freeze Frame - J. Geils Band

It's Monday morning and I just walked out of Scripps Hospital Imaging Building where I had a CT scan done. I've been looking forward to this. This is the very last thing I have to do before extraction. Ahhh, feels so nice to say that. Think I'll say it twice. This is the very last test. Very last. It's sooo very last. I took the earliest appointment possible and did it in San Diego. Still got my pedal to the metal.

I showed up 15 minutes early as requested, filled out some paperwork, and obtained the ceremonial medical bracelet on my wrist. This signifies to everyone that I belong. Then I waited around forever. I think they were probably running 45 minutes late. Apparently, they didn't get the memo that this was my last test in a marathon of tests needed for approval.

I finally got in and saw a technician named Ansel. Ansel was my kind of dude and made the wait worth it. It was easy getting to know him. He asked me about what I was doing and why he was going to take pictures of my innards. I told him, and he was like, wow, I really admire that. Really great.

The whole time, he was totally chumming with me, hitting me on the shoulder and stuff, you know. And then some woman put me in a chair, and they put this warm blanket on me. Like fresh out of the hot dryer warm. So good! But then they tied the rubber balloon thing around my bicep and started looking for a spot to insert a needle. Funny thing, I thought I was done with needles until surgery. WRONG!

This woman stuck a needle in me for (I hope) the last time. Then I just waited there until Ansel was ready for me. When it was my turn, they took me into a room with a giant machine. Pants off, underwear on, hop on machine. Basically, they just ran me through the machine up and down and it took a bunch of images.

The reason they put the needle line in my arm was so they could pump some dye into me and then take more pictures with the machine. Ansel was in another room, talking to me through an intercom. I think he was in there because the behemoth scanner I was laying in was omitting 1.21-gigawatt gamma rays, which is enough to shrink your head. That, or he was worried that the dye line going into my arm would get loose and spray the place.

Ansel said, "Okay, things are gonna get warm." A moment later I knew the dye was going in, but I couldn't feel it. Then the strangest warming sensation engulfed my ears and my head. Super weird. Then I felt warmth down in my southern region. Whoa.

Ansel and I were talking the whole time about all kinds of stuff. He's a hockey guy and he was pumped when I told him that my son, Jeremiah, plays. We talked a little bit about special needs, because if you talk to me long enough, that's where the conversation is headed. When the scanning was over, it was time to dig for info.

Me: So how does everything look?

Ansel: I'm just a technician.

Me: You see the images?

Ansel: Yeah.

Me: Well?

Ansel: I'm just a technician.

Me: Oh, come on man, you see these things all the time. Are there two kidneys?

Ansel: Yeah.

Me: Tell me more.

Ansel: Everything's fantastic. You're going to be the best donor anyone ever had.

Me: That's what I'm talking about.

Ansel: They are the best kidneys I've ever seen. This is the greatest. You're gonna be a great donor. You know, she's got the best donor she could ever hope for.

When he said that last statement, he put his hands on my shoulders, and I thought he was going to hug me. It was a pretty cool experience meeting a guy who was sincere like that. I probably needed a little boost. As I walked out the door, Ansel said, "I'm rooting for you, man. I'm really rooting for you and I'm rooting for the girl who's getting your kidney. This is a great thing."

It was a touching moment. I am finally done. It's done. I decided not to call Steve Petersen to tell him that I just found out that I've got the best kidneys in the world, and I've got the pictures to prove it. Instead, I called the University of Utah. I asked for Nurse

Teresa, but she was not there. Then I asked for Nurse Downer; she wasn't there either. I did, however, get Nurse Nightingale.. I said, "I'm done here. You should have the results tomorrow. Any chance we can go to the board Thursday?" She said "sure" and that all signs looked good to be presented and approved by the board this Thursday. I felt triumphant and tired, like I just won a distance race.

I fired off this email to Nurse Teresa:

From: Rick Daynes
To: Nurse Teresa
Date: 03/12/2018 2:33 pm
Subject: DONE

Hi Teresa,

I completed my CT scan this morning. They said results should be in tomorrow. Please let me know if I passed. And if so, will you be able to present my case to the board on Thursday? I also called and reported to Nightingale. But I forgot to ask her if I could send the CT scan results to my doc. Is that doable?

Thanks,

Rick

March 14, 2018

2 Legit 2 Quit - MC Hammer

Now it's Wednesday. I got a call from Nurse Teresa at the transplant center. Of course, I am fully expecting a stellar review and report of my CT scan. Teresa is going to gush about how great my kidneys look and tell me how prepared she is for tomorrow's meeting, how the presentation will be off the charts, and that the board is sure to approve my kidney donation.

That's what I was thinking. But...yet again, there was another fire to put out. Nurse Teresa informed me that they have yet to see my CT scans. My heart started to beat fast and I'm like, great, another hoop to jump through. Tomorrow, my case is supposed to be presented to the board. No pictures, no presentation.

On Monday, when I had the CT, the guy at the front desk said the transplant center should get the results in one to two days. And Ansel said they would have it the next day. Because of that, I didn't think anything of it. I didn't follow up or do anything. I thought it was out of my hands. But of course, it wasn't. Why should I expect hospitals to communicate with each other? The orders were from the University of Utah Transplant Department. Why didn't Sharp in San Diego simply email the pics to them right away? I took another break from work and started making calls.

The only number I had for Sharp was for scheduling. I called and got a hold of... I think her name was Flipper? She was the woman who I called to begin with, the one I scheduled my original appointment with. This was only a week ago. Remember, I still had my pedal to the metal. I said, "My name is Rick Daynes. I scheduled an appointment with you..." She remembered me. I explained the situation and then she told me I needed to call the imaging department. I said I didn't have a number, so she gave me one and

I called it immediately. It was a fax machine. No good. I called her back and got a better number... I hoped.

I called the new number and got the guy at the front desk, the same guy who told me the transplant center would have the images in one to two days. I gave him the two second version of why I was calling. He looked in the files and told me that for some reason, the images were not sent.

I said, "Well, can you send them over now?" He said "Okay, but we have to put the images on a disk and mail them." I replied, "Uh. No, you don't. It's 2018 and you can simply email them or electronically transmit them in several different ways. It's easy." Then he tells me he can't because of some policy or something. Now I'm back in fight mode. Another issue, another deadline, it's a recurring theme in my quest to do this thing! But you know what else is a recurring theme? Winning. I will win this game because I have no quit. I'm too legit to quit.

Me: You told me on Monday that the University of Utah would have the images in one to two days. They were supposed to have the images already. My case is supposed to be presented tomorrow morning.

Dude at the desk: I'm really sorry about this man.

Me: Let's figure out a solution. I'm willing to do anything I need to get those images to them. What would be the quickest way to do that?

Dude: Well, there are actually two things here. The images and a report.

Me: Your people made a report on what it looks like?

Dude: Yep. I can fax the report, but the only way I can legally send the images is to put them on a disk and mail it.

Me: Okay, I will get a fax number for you. Can you overnight the images?

Dude: Yes

Me: I'll call you right back.

I then called Teresa at the Transplant Center.

Me: Hi Teresa. Scripps is going to fax the report over. Do you still need the images if you have a full report?

Teresa: Yes, we cannot rely on the report. We have to review the images.

Me: But they will not electronically transfer them to you. They will overnight them, and you'll have them tomorrow morning.

Teresa: In order for your case to be presented, our people need to review the images today and prepare our own report so the case can be presented tomorrow.

Me: SHOOT! Okay, new plan. I'll drive down to Sharp. They are images of me, right? So, shouldn't they be able to give me the images? They are pictures of me! If I get the disk, I can get to my office and then I will electronically transfer them to you. But will you accept that? Will you accept it? Coming from me, the guy whose images you're reading?

Teresa: I don't know, but I'll find out.

Our conversation ended and I was hopping! I was also hoping! I was a hopping hoper! I gave the dude at the desk the fax number with instructions to write "Attention: Nurse Teresa" on it. He started the faxing process while I asked the big question. "Dude, if I come to you, can you give me the disk with the images?" His answer was in the affirmative and I literally ran to my car while telling him I was on my way.

Nurse Teresa called back while I was screaming down the freeway. The day was growing short.

Me: Hi! Did you find out if you can accept the images from me?

Teresa: I don't know. Still working on that, but we did get the report they faxed over.

Me: Cool, what does it say?

Teresa: I don't see any red flags in the report.

Me: Sweet!

Teresa: You do have a hernia.

Me: WHAT THE..!?

Teresa: You have a hernia. It's right underneath your belly button.

Me: You gotta be kidding me!

Teresa: Nope.

Me: And that's not a red flag?

Teresa: It shouldn't be a problem. We'll ask the surgeons if they'll go ahead and repair that as long as they are in there.

We hung up. She knew I was racing to get the images, so she was trying to get an answer. The hernia thing was weird and unexpected, but not a total shocker. I have six brothers and all of them have had a hernia. Half of them have had two hernias. My dad had a hernia and even my mom had one. I had begun to wonder if I was adopted or switched at birth. I will wonder no more.

Teresa called back pretty fast with bad news. They could not accept the images from me. TOTAL BUMMER! I was out of options and I had lost this battle. The case would not be presented tomorrow. I had to wait another week. I called the Dude at the desk and asked him to mail the disk. Profanity is not in my vernacular, but if there ever was a time to let something fly, it was then.

I cannot believe I missed another Thursday for my case to be presented. It seems like this should have been done months ago. The emotional turmoil of this whole thing has just been crazy. Today was nuts, in part, because I thought I was done with this whole process two days ago! Then, I learned today that I still have the fire. I still have the fuel. I can see the Petersens sitting there, reserved, not letting themselves get excited. Honestly, as I said before, Jenny will not accept that this is happening until there is a kidney in a silver dish next to her while she's laying on the operating table, or she wakes up with one inside of her.

March 16, 2018

Update I sent to my family:

Kidney Update
Rick Daynes
Fri 3/16/2018 5:45 AM

Thought I'd give a kidney update. Basically, the roller coaster continues. Frankly, I'm pretty sick of all the hoops and having everything that could possibly go wrong, go wrong. The very last thing to get done was my CT scan, which I did Monday morning at Scripps in La Jolla. Not the beach, but the medical center. It was weak and sweet at the same time. Images and results were supposed to be at the U Tuesday so my case could be presented to the board on Thursday. But of course, they did not get the results Tuesday or Wednesday or Thursday. So, I went several rounds with Scripps yesterday and at one point was in my car driving down there to slap some records people around when I thought better of it.

The good news is that, so far, there are no red flags on the CT scan. This comes from the report that accompanies it. And even better news. The scan revealed that I have a HERNIA! I AM RELATED TO YOU! All these years of wondering if I was switched at birth when they put me in the room with 90 other babies can now be put to rest. They said I have probably had it my whole life.I have already put in a request for the U doctors to fix it as long as they are in there. Stay tuned. If you need something to pray for, it is that the images will get to the U. Thursday is the day the kidney board gets together and reviews the candidate and stamps it approved or denied. I'm hoping to share that sweet moment with my bros, surfing a sweet right point break.

L8

Rick

March 20, 2018

If This Is It - Huey Lewis

It's Tuesday and I haven't heard anything from the Transplant Center, so I called Nurse Teresa and left a message. I did not hear back, so chances are that she is not working. I did get a hold of Nurse Nightingale, but she was busy. She told me there was a lot going on.

[Note to self: Tuesday is transplant day so not the best day for me to be bugging people about my status. I should have followed up every day since my scan!]

So, I just said to Nightingale, "Look, I just need to know if the images are in and if they look good and if my case is being presented on Thursday." We hung up and I heard nothing back.

I got a text today from Steve that Jenny's latest test results came in and it's not good. Her creatinen is now 5.73 and kidney function is at 8%. Last month, her kidney function was at 10%. The downward trend continues. I texted him back and asked if he could talk.

We then talked on the phone for about 30 minutes. I told him about the CT scan and that I hoped the case would be presented to the board on Thursday. I asked him, "If I get approved, should we move the date up? You know, get in there as soon as possible?" He said he thought we should, and that they would ask their doctor.

How can you live with your only kidney functioning at 8%? How is that even possible? I'm wondering if their doc is going to tell them it's time for dialysis. They have been avoiding dialysis like the plague. And that's a good thing. Dialysis is never good.

March 21, 2018

Sincerely, Me - Dear Evan Hansen

Today is Wednesday. Of course, it's Wednesday! The day before my case is presented to the board. Once again, I have not learned my lesson! Also, I have been just plain busy. I have not received word about my case. This is concerning to say the least. I shot off another email to Teresa.

From: Rick Daynes
To: Nurse Teresa
Date: 03/21/2018 9:09 AM
Subject: Will I be presented tomorrow?

Good Morning Teresa!

I know you are busy. I just need to know two things. 1. Have my images been reviewed and how do they look? 2. Is everything in order for my case to be presented to the board tomorrow?

Jenny, my potential recipient, has dropped to 8% kidney function and 5.73 creatinine. We really need to find out if I am the donor. If they need to go back to the drawing board, best to find out soon.

Thanks!

Rick Daynes

From: Nurse Teresa
To: Rick Daynes
Date: 03/21/2018 10:12 AM
Subject: RE: Will I be presented tomorrow?

Rick,

Good morning. I will be reviewing your CT scan today with Dr. Harvest. If he says it looks good, then yes, I will present your case tomorrow. With Jenny's kidney function dropping, are you wanting to donate sooner if possible?

Teresa

From: Rick Daynes
To: Nurse Teresa
Date: 03/21/2018 10:44 AM
Subject: RE: Will I be presented tomorrow?

I think the answer to that question is yes. However, I am not discussing schedules or anything with them until I know I'm approved. Thanks for your efforts and I'm looking forward to a scan result later today.

Thanks,

Rick

From: Nurse Teresa
To: Rick Daynes
Date: 03/21/2018 12:43 pm
Subject: RE: Will I be presented tomorrow?

Rick,

We reviewed the scans, nothing abnormal. Dr.
Harvest would prefer to use your left kidney. I will call
you after I present tomorrow

Nurse Teresa

March 21, 2018: Evening

Don't Fear the Reaper - Blue Oyster Cult

I touched base with Steve Petersen a few times today.
You would think that we would all be electrified with
the news that my case will be presented to the board
tomorrow for final approval. You would think that.
Honestly though, we were waiting for something
demoralizing to happen. Every time we get to a good
point, like right now, something comes crashing down.

Getting an email from Teresa saying the doc wanted
to take my left kidney was a bit surreal. When she
wrote that she would call me tomorrow after she
presented my case to the board, that was unearthly. Is
it really happening? Is it really done? All the

paperwork is in. All the tests are done. All the sticks. All the urine. All the blood. All the scans. All the education. All the X-rays. All the interviews. All the emails and phone calls. All the EVERYTHING! You name it, and it is done. My case is being presented tomorrow.

I copied and pasted Nurse Teresa's email and sent it to Steve and Jenny. I couldn't simply forward it because it's in the hospital's communication site. I got a couple of replies back from Steve, all sarcastic, funny stuff.

For example, "Rick. Jenny and I are both left-handed. So, we are more than stoked with the left kidney." Then a couple political jabs that Jenny will lean too far left with a left kidney "#Hillary2020." And the wisecracks kept coming.

I wonder how they are really feeling. Jenny, no doubt, is suppressing all thoughts and emotions but praying like her life depends on it. Because it does.

TOMORROW IS A BIG DAY.

March 22, 2018

We Are the Champions - Queen

Last night, I drove up to Camp Pendleton and checked into a cottage on the beach at San Onofre. My brothers and I, along with Nate Seaman, try to do this every year. We watch the March Madness Basketball tournament and surf all day. I woke up this morning and it was raining, but the surf was fantastic.

After our dawn patrol session, I told everyone I was gonna go to the temple. My brother- in-law, D.J., and my brother Steve jumped in my van, and we went to the Newport Beach temple. It's a beautiful temple and it was a special time. Nothing like being in a sacred place on a special day, petitioning God for mercy.

At 2:00 PM, we were on our way back to the cottage and I was wondering why I had not heard from Nurse Teresa. My case was presented to the board in the morning. Why the delay? For some reason, despite all the set-backs, I did not have any bad feelings or thoughts. I felt calm and knew that the call would come soon.

We pulled out of the Costco parking lot with some grub and a full tank of gas. The phone started ringing and I had no clue where it was. I told DJ and Steve to follow the sound of the ring and find my phone. I just knew it was Teresa. I had told everyone the day before that my case was going before the board today. I would either be approved or denied. So, DJ and Steve knew what I was talking about.

Sure enough, my cell was sliding around on the floor between surfboards and wetsuits. DJ found it and I pulled over. Teresa said, "Hey, I just wanted to tell you, congratulations, you have been approved." It was just like that! It was really done. I was really going to do this. I was really giving a kidney.

I could not be more thankful for Nurse Teresa, and I told her so. I said, "Thank you so much. I know this has been a different kind of trip for you. With everything failing and then not failing…" She agreed it was really different than any process she had been through before and we talked about the iothalamate test being so crazy. Then she said, "But, you know, everything looks good and you're ready to go." Then she wanted to talk about a date. I said, " [The Petersens] are going to have a meeting with their nephrologists and go over that. So, I will let you know as soon as they come up with a date." Then I called Steve and told him I just got a call from the U:

Steve: Yeah, what'd they say?

Me: They said, congratulations, you've been approved.

Steve: Oh, yay!

We talked briefly about coming up with a date. I told him again that my goal was to get to this point as soon as possible. The ball was now in their court.

I then called Robin. It was kind of anticlimactic. Robin was sleeping, plus I had my brother Steve and DJ in the car. I told her it was all approved, it was really happening now. It was really happening. I said, "yes, all we need to do is set a date, go in and do it. That's it. I mean, I haven't had the operation yet. But I pray that I'll get in better shape and be strong and that I'll be able to recover well."

We got back to the beach, and I told everyone else. Nothing but good vibes and support and sarcasm. Just what I expected. Conditions were a little stormy, but the surf was super fun. Especially fun to surf and hang with my brothers. Ozz was there and I told him everything that had happened. He was stoked. Shoots, we were all stoked.

Can I talk about spiritual matters for a minute? I did not hear a voice or see an angel or a sign or feel an overwhelming burning that I was called to give this family a life-saving organ. I did pray a lot. I fasted. And I felt really good about doing this. To me, it was God approving a decision I had made. I studied it out. I listened and sought understanding and I took it to the Lord. He has assured me many times during this journey that this is the right thing to do.

There were times when I doubted. Times when I would spin things in my mind or feel a little anxiety. My faith fluctuates. But through every test, whether I passed or failed, I could see the hand of the Lord supporting this and allowing it to happen. It did not happen the way I wanted it to. It was not easy, convenient, or painless. By painless, I am not talking about the needles. Well, I mean, I am a little tired of being stuck. I am talking about the emotions of life and the virtual hills and valleys that our team has driven through to get to this point. Life's greatest lessons and blessings do not come easy; I bank them every chance I get.

The following is an email we received from Jenny Petersen tonight.

Dear Rick and Robin,

As the news of the day is settling in, I can't let the night go without thanking you for getting us to this point. (And any words I come up with feel completely inadequate!) Thank you for dealing with and enduring all the testing, for constantly pushing the U along, and for your unwavering persistence throughout the ups and downs. I think you are both remarkable people to be willing to do this for someone you barely know, sacrificing so much for my benefit. As my kidney is now declining a bit more rapidly, you've provided a significant measure of peace to us and our kids that things will work out. Your family has been in our prayers constantly, and I just hope the Lord has some extra special blessings in store for you!

With gratitude,

Jenny

March 23, 2018

My reply to Jenny's email:

Fri 3/23/2018 6:31 AM

Jenny,

The Lord is way ahead of you. He's already blessed us tremendously. And this will no doubt be another blessing for us as well as for you and your sweet family. Honestly, we are grateful to be in a position where we can help. We cannot imagine what you have endured, getting to this point, and are grateful that you feel peace. You mentioned once that you felt there was a time clock on your life. Well, you can throw that clock away because there is a big, healthy, fully functioning, long lasting, APPROVED kidney in the on-deck circle.

All the Best!

Rick

April 15, 2018

No Surprises - Radiohead

Surprise entry today. And the surprise is there is no surprise. Not a lot to report really. Well, except for the armchair quarterback in my head, speculating. It has been a little more than three weeks since I got approved. Wouldn't you think we'd have a surgery date by now?

Here is what I do know:

1. The Petersens were hoping for surgery this fall. Get the kids back in school and busy. It would be less burdensome on childcare. I was also hoping for a fall date or even later. Fall is my slow season at work and to recover while watching football is appealing. However...

2. Jenny's kidney ain't getting any better. She has been in a steady decline for a long time and my last report was that Jenny's one functioning kidney was performing at a meager 8%. I did not know you could be alive at that number.

3. We all know Jenny is not going to make it to the fall.

4. We all know the surgery dates are going fast. May and June are no longer options.

5. I am officially approved by the board, which means I passed the ball to the pros. They have 10 seconds to get that ball past the half court line, and they ain't moving.

April 26, 2018

I Can See Clearly Now - Johnny Nash

I just got back from speaking at the biggest and best special education conference in the United States. The conference was in Dallas, and I was the Monday night keynote speaker. It was awesome and also pretty stressful, but I'm back now, with a clear head and back to planning for the future.

I was approved for the transplant over a month ago and with things the way they are, I could not help but think about the halt in action. I moved as fast as I could to get approved. Now, I had nothing to do. I was stagnant, playing the waiting game, and it felt abnormal.

There was something else on my mind. The solution was here, but I was wondering if stage fright had set in, and Jenny couldn't pull the trigger. I was ready to donate and Jenny was ready to expire. I am only speculating here, but I think Jenny might be stalling. Pretty sure she is stalling. She's definitely stalling. I think she has cold feet and does not want to take my kidney. She probably never thought we would get to this point. Now that we are here, it's difficult. But the alternative is dialysis followed by more health problems and an early death.

Nurse Teresa happened to phone as I was contemplating this. It was another sign, and it was as clear to me as a blitzing linebacker who wants everyone to know he's coming.

Me: Teresa, when is the next available date we can do the surgery?

Teresa: July and August are pretty full, but I do have two openings at the end of July and one on July 3rd.

Me: July 3rd. Book it.

Teresa: You sure? Do you want to call them and discuss it?

Me: Nope. Book it. What could be better than watching the Fourth of July fireworks from the roof of the hospital? If we need to cancel, I will call you back later today.

Teresa: Are you going to tell them?

Me: Yep, if they are not good with it, I will call you right back. I just want to be locked in with a date.

Teresa: I have Daynes and Petersens down for July 3rd kidney transplant.

I called Steve two seconds later and told him I made a bold move and scheduled the surgery. I said that dates were going fast so I pulled the trigger. July 3rd was the next available day, and it works for me. I asked him to get back to me soon if that date did not work for them. No doubt about it—Steve was happy I had grabbed a date.

I then called Robin and cleared it with her. Then it was off to making plans.

April 27, 2018

Hotel Motel Holiday Inn - Rapper's Delight

I have a super cool aunt and uncle who previously invited me to stay and recuperate at their place post-surgery. I shot them the following:

From: Rick Daynes
To: Uncle Rob and Aunt Connie
Date: Fri 4/27/2018 8:41 AM
Subject: Are you Kidney Me?

Hey T.O. and Connie,

Surgery is officially scheduled for July 3rd. Tentative schedule is (and I am making this up now): Probably fly in a couple days prior. Check into Draper luxury accommodations [their house], go hang with Ozz and kidney recipient's family and chill for a couple days.

Tuesday early morning: check into the U hospital.

Thursday: probably get released and back to your Casita. Could be a day earlier or later, depending on how I'm doing.

Nurse Robin will stay with me for probably a few more days and train T.O., who will then take over as head nurse. I hope I don't need to do more than watch a movie or two or 20. Stay two-ish weeks and then fly back to SD. Talk that over. I do have other options, including hotel accommodations that we don't have to pay for. That's a long time to house me. I'm going to mess up the pillows and you guys could be on OCD overload. So, I am giving you the opportunity to back out and we'll still be BFF's

Talk to you later,

Rick

May 4, 2018

Talk To Me - Stevie Nicks

And a very happy May the 4th be with you! You know, I consider myself a pretty good leader. And I say that because I believe a large part of leadership is following up. I learned at a young age that if you dished out an assignment and didn't follow up to make sure it was done, there would be a good chance it wouldn't be. Not that I am the one dishing out the assignments in the carousel of my kidney saga, but I could have done a better job, especially on this last chapter with the scan. I missed the first Thursday because I figured the CT would get there in plenty of time. Yeah, and I barely made it the next Thursday. I'm going to make it a point to follow up more. So, to make sure everything was a go, I sent Teresa this:

From: Rick Daynes
To: Nurse Teresa
Date: 05/04/2018 11:27 am
Subject: Following Up

Hi Teresa,

Just to confirm. We are scheduled for kidney transplant July 3rd, second surgery of the day.

Also, I wanted to see if you had heard anything about repairing my hernia, as long as they were in there.

Thanks,

Rick Daynes

May 22, 2018

Spirit In the Sky - Norman Greenbaum

I'm in Hawaii and it is time to get religious again. The scriptures talk about gifts of the spirit. To one is given this and to another is given that. The idea that people have gifts given from God hits home for me. Having kids with special needs has taught me to have an open mind. When your children struggle, you'll look into all kinds of things you previously would not have touched. I think having this openness and seeing progress has broadened my perspective on spiritual matters. I'm in Hawaii on a business trip, but also to see my friend, Kimo Kahuna, who has the gift of healing.

I just got a blessing from Kimo. Before the blessing, we talked about the rejection of the kidney. Kimo said that the only problem with kidneys is that when people are harboring resentment, that's when their kidneys go bad. Kidneys are directly connected to forgiveness. If you can forgive, you're going to have great kidneys.

He gave me several examples of people that he has counseled, including a man named Kai Kekoa. There was a person in his life that he wouldn't forgive, and he was having kidney problems because of it. Kimo told me that I needed to talk to Jenny because if she were harboring any issues, she would continue to have problems. I said I would.

Then Kimo gave me such a powerful blessing. He told me that Heavenly Father would bless me immensely for my sacrifice. He said that Heavenly Father was proud that I was charitable and willing to sacrifice myself for the good of others. He blessed me and Jenny to have good recoveries. He said that there wouldn't be any problems and that the Lord would open up towards that. Doors would open up that would bless all of our lives immensely.

I feel like that's really true. And I also feel like He'll bless me for donating. But I'm not doing it because I'll be blessed. I'm doing it because it's the right thing to do. That's who I am. Kimo also said that my wife and my kids would be blessed because of my actions. It was a wonderful blessing.

I have faith in Kimo's blessing and have no doubt this will be fantastic. I'll have a good recovery and all the blessings Kimo mentioned will be poured upon my family. All is good. All as well. By the end of the blessing, I was crying. I hugged Kimo; he is such a gracious and powerful man.

June 1, 2018

More Than Words - Extreme

A few days ago, my friend Ashley stopped me to ask about my upcoming kidney donation. I was caught off guard, as I did not think that cat was out of the bag. It was weird, like we were meant to run into each other.

Her father is waiting for a lung donation, and she is helping to keep him alive. I emailed her afterwards.

From: Rick Daynes
To: Ashley
Date: 06/01/2018 2:16 pm
Subject: Thanks

Hi Ashley!

I just wanted to say thanks. I feel like God put you in my path on Sunday when you stopped me to talk about my upcoming kidney donation. I had only mentioned it to my priesthood leaders and to one other member of the ward. Pretty sure Robin has told a few people as well, so I did not know if word was out. So, congratulations, you are the first to ask me about it, and I really needed it! Ever since then, I have been thinking about our family's experience with this and the recipient's family, and wondering if this is something to share.

I think the answer is YES. Robin and I had that moment years ago when we decided we were not going to be a special needs reclusive family any longer and we were going to talk about our real issues and how we deal with them. Well, I now feel the same way about this kidney thing. Five thousand people die every year waiting for a kidney. If I can help by talking about it, I'm in.

I needed to have a little introspection and see if I'm up for beating the donation drum. Your family is no stranger to organ donation, so it's fitting that my little self-examination should start with you.

Thanks Ashley!

Rick

Boom Boom Pow - Black Eyed Peas

I grew up with some great guys. I don't keep in touch with them, but I don't keep in touch with a lot of people. I decided to dig them up on Facebook and put a group chat together. I sent this message to Dave Riley, Andrew Miller, Lance Martineau, Trevor Rogers, and Derryl Acosta (my "Sandlot friends").

Dear Sandlot Friends,

I suppose I should say Stand by Me friends, because I think we watched that movie as much as any. I have a request. I am donating a kidney to a friend soon. Doctor says my life with one kidney will be the same except for one thing, absolutely no contact sports. I haven't played a contact sport in 20 years, so life will be the same. But then I got thinking, I will no longer have the option.

My boys just finished rugby season and I've been telling them stories about British Bulldog, vince and slugs, middle, punchbug, full contact three flies up, etc. They're like, "So dad, you and your friends would just smack each other all the time?" I think it was an important part of growing up that kids now have no idea about. When was the last time you saw kids playing a pick-up game of tackle football? So here is my request.

To officially end my career in contact sports, I want to play one last game of British Bulldog at the Grossmont building. I know we're old and run down, but I want to stick and get stuck on the lawn where it all started. This is where we cut our teeth and I'd like to go back there for one last grass stain.

So, what do you say? If I can get you guys, then maybe reach out to others. Plus, I have three teenagers who need to experience this.

Rick

June 17, 2018

Everybody Hurts - R.E.M.

It was great connecting with the guys I grew up with. Most were on board and I recruited my brothers, sons, and some other old friends. Nurse Robin, however, found out about it and put an abrupt stop to the entire thing. She said that by going out there and risking any kind of injury, I was putting my surgery at risk. The entire process I'd been fighting for could be stopped or delayed by one stupid injury. And all because I wanted to tackle someone for the last time. She's right of course, and just like that my full contact sports career came to an end.

Doctor! Doctor! – Thompson Twins

Today is Tuesday. Last Thursday, I had a cold. No big deal. I usually fight through colds pretty fast, especially this year. For example, when Eli came home with a stomach bug, it worked its way to Tyler, Robin, Summer, and Jefferson (Jeremiah never got it). I got it, but fought it off well and never threw up.

So back to last Thursday and the cold. Friday, it was no big deal. Saturday, I still had it. Sunday was the worst day. Monday, I kind of felt better and thought that the cold was on its way out. That afternoon I felt like, oh, yeah, I'm getting better, and I will be 90% tomorrow.

I woke up at 3:30 AM this morning (Tuesday) because Eli was up and was playing in the family room. He had turned on all the lights in the entire house except for the bedrooms. He was courteous enough to close all the bedroom doors so people could sleep while he played. Did I mention it was 3:30 in the morning? I got up and put him back in bed and laid down with him. Long story short, I could not sleep, and I realized I was still sick. Around 6:00 AM, I figured I probably should talk to my doctor about this nagging cold. I emailed Dr. Jellyfinger.

Date: 06/19/2018 7:16 am

Subject: Surgery Sick

Hi Doc and possibly Goodtidings, two weeks from today, I am donating my kidney. One week from tomorrow, I have my last labs. All systems are go, except for one thing. I am sick. I have been healthy for a long time and now I've been sick since last Thursday. I'm sure it's just a cold, but sometimes it feels like the flu. Yesterday, I felt better and thought I would be maybe 90% today. But I'm not. Normally, I wouldn't bother you and let nature run its course, but I've got surgery approaching. Your thoughts?

Thanks,

Rick Daynes

The reply came back quickly as usual:

Date: 06/19/2018 7:56 am
Subject: RE: Surgery Sick

Hi Rick, I have made you an appointment for today with Dr Jellyfinger at 2:50 PM so that he can evaluate you. Let us know if that does not work.

Goodtidings

My reply:

Date: 06/19/2018 8:05 am
Subject: RE: RE: RE: Surgery Sick

Thank you, I'll be there.

Rick

At 2:50 PM, I rolled into Jellyfinger's office. I was still scarred from the prostate incident. I wondered if things would be awkward between us.

Nurse Goodtidings, the same Goodtidings who inadvertently told me that I was going to have a son with Down Syndrome, took my vitals. She told me my oxygen saturation level was at 94%. I told her, "I mostly feel fine. I'm just paranoid because of the surgery in two weeks." She says, "Yeah, well, your oxygen saturation is at 94."

A few minutes later, Dr. Jellyfinger walked in. He listened to my lungs and told me I had wheezing going on all over the place. He spent some time looking at a computer screen. He kept scrolling down and down and then said he thinks he knows what is going on. The only problem is he cannot see what he is looking for in my chart. He asked me if I ever had childhood asthma.

I said, "Yeah. When I was a kid, I played Pop Warner football, and I was wheezing like crazy when I ran. My parents made me feel like it was a psychological thing, or I was allergic to the grass or something like that." He told me I definitely had asthma. I asked him why he was bringing that up now. He said, "You never get rid of asthma. It's a virus that's always with you. Just because it never comes up doesn't mean it's gone."

I was totally floored. I asked, "So I have asthma?" He said, "You have asthma, and your asthma is allergic to this cold. Your asthma, even though you never feel it, has flared up." It was super interesting to find out I still had asthma and that it could flare up when I caught a cold or for whatever reason.

Then the doc played out this scenario. He said, "If you really want to have this surgery, we've got to have a full court press." I said, "Absolutely." He told me,

"Here's what we're gonna do..." And he laid out a plan. Then he called the University of Utah and asked them if there were any problems about giving me certain steroids to get everything back and rolling in the right way.

Then I went to get a chest X-ray to see if I had pneumonia. That came back clean. Yea! No pneumonia! They then sent me to get an inhaler, an oral antibiotic, and a steroid. Jellyfinger ordered me not to do any exercises and to come back on Monday. How's that for a full court press?

Couple thoughts:

Yesterday, I was supposed to go on a high adventure with my son, Tyler, and his scout troop. I made the commitment six months ago. Even when surgery was scheduled, I was still going to go because I figured I could still get my work done—and what better way to get in shape for this surgery? Today, we would have been at 8,000 feet in elevation, hiking 10 miles with a pack. Tomorrow, another 10 miles and Thursday, another 10 miles. Friday is whitewater rafting and it's all at high altitude in the High Sierra Nevada Mountain Range.

At the last minute, I bailed. I did not feel the spirit tell me to do this. Or did I? Was this part of God's plan? If I had gone up there with Tyler, there would be no surgery. I would not have been able to do it. I would have been the liability, the casualty. I probably would have ended up in a hospital. Wouldn't that have been a good time? This is just one more thing in this crazy string of events leading up to this surgery. And it is one more sign telling me that God is in charge.

But wait, there's more! My family is having a family reunion in Bicknell, Utah starting tomorrow and going for five days. My wife and other kids are there. This is also at altitude in the middle of nowhere and includes hiking and all sorts of physical activities. I could have driven to the transplant center following the reunion. Think there wasn't pressure to attend that? And yet I bailed on that too!

For those of you keeping score at home. Let's recap:

1. I bailed on the Daynes family reunion even though my wife and kids went. The reunion was in Utah, and it would have been easy to drive to the medical center for surgery following the reunion.

2. I bailed on a high adventure backpacking and river raft trip that I committed to go on with my son.

3. Had I attended either of the two previous events, I wouldn't be giving a kidney on our scheduled date. I would have been sick and possibly hospitalized.

4. Two weeks before my scheduled kidney donation, I got a cold that set off my asthma.

5. I haven't had asthma since I was in fourth grade and did not really know I had it.

6. If I did not go see my doctor today and get on his full court press, I would not be giving a kidney at our scheduled date.

7. In addition to the new inhaler and drugs, I was ordered to rest, which I do not do well and is impossible to do when my family is home.

8. My family is not home.

June 22, 2018

Call Me - Blondie

I got a call today from the Transplant Center. I am not the best at answering my cell these days unless I know it is important or it's the Transplant Center. As soon as I see the 801-area code, I answer ASAP. This time, when I answered, it was Nurse Nightingale. Nurse Teresa only works two days a week in the Transplant Center, so they all have to share the load. They are a good team. Despite all the issues and the funky lab tests, they have been really good to work with.

Nightingale told me that I needed to take labs one last time. This sounded familiar. I am pretty sure I already celebrated my final labs and jabs, but now that I think about it, I do remember something about doing one more set of labs just before surgery to make sure everything was still cool. Nightingale sent the orders to my local lab and now I have my final, final labs next Wednesday.

Nightingale and I also talked briefly about the coming week and a half, and she asked when I was flying to Salt Lake. I told her that Robin and I would be landing the day before the surgery. She told me that I would get a call the day before surgery as to what time I

147

should check in. I already knew that one of those times was early and the other was ludicrously early; I was hoping for the former. She asked me a few more questions about lodging and preparation. During our conversation, she kept asking if I needed anything or had any questions about anything and, if I did, to give her a call. She said her line was open and she was ready to assist. You see what I'm sayin'? This was a good team, ready to help in any way.

June 24, 2018

Times Like These - Foo Fighters

Today is Sunday, my last week with two kidneys. It's late at night and I can't sleep. So let me recap a couple of things:

I had a conversation with Steve Petersen a couple days ago. He said, "Hey, I just wanted to tell you that the scheduling was pure genius." He said that there was no way that Jenny could hang on any longer. I mean, there was just no way. He told me that he and Jenny went to an event, and they had to walk up this hill. It took Jenny forever to get up it. She was not doing well. And so, he thanked me for taking matters into my own hands and for scheduling the earliest possible time, which, again, is July 3rd.

Steve said they were having another ward fast for Jenny, me, and my family. They would ask that our family be blessed and that I be blessed. He asked me if there was anything I would like to add. That is pretty powerful, huh? An entire congregation, fasting for us? And he is asking if I want to add anything to the fast?

148

Of course, being me, I poked fun at his question and asked for superpowers. Maybe laser vision or flight would be cool. Steve said he didn't think anything was off the table.

That was cool and it was fun to tell Robin about it. It's always fun to tell Robin about everything. I don't think there is a single detail that I have not shared with my wife. It's where I go to make sure I am doing everything right. It is where I go for comfort when I need it.

The closer we get to the actual event, the closer I feel to God. I have really been feeling the spirit a lot lately. Just feeling it. Feeling good and occasionally having a good cry. Today at church, taking the Sacrament was a really good experience. I could not stop crying. I feel closer to the Savior because I'm giving of myself. I feel more selfless and more clear-headed.

Our lesson today was about the loaves and the fishes. Such a great story, in which Jesus fed the masses both spiritually and physically. It is a wonderful lesson in kindness and compassion. I could not help but think that I am giving Jenny what she needs physically. It is a selfless act of kindness and compassion. The Lord will provide for both of us.

I had emailed the bishop this morning to tell him my recipient's ward was having a fast for me, my family, and the Petersens. I told him I was thinking about asking the brethren if they'd include me in their fast. He asked me if we should include the relief society? I said I just felt comfortable with the men. I'm not sure why. It feels a little self-promoting. Here I am doing a selfless act and now I am telling everyone, "Hey everybody, I'm doing this selfless thing!"

It does feel comforting and empowering to have friends, family, and strangers pray and fast for you. No doubt about it. There is strength in that. Bishop Walton stopped me and said, "if you're okay with it, I'd like to announce it to the brethren. I said I was okay with that.

When Bishop Walton finished with all the announcements, he said, "Next week, Rick Daynes will be donating a kidney. I would like to ask that you include him in your thoughts and prayers and in your fast next Sunday." That was it.

I have a lot of good friends in that group of brothers and most of them had no idea about the donation, so it really took them by surprise. Guys were like, "What?!" And a lot of chirping started about it. Dave Bagley then got up and asked if I could say anything about it, since no one knew what was going on.

I got up and gave a brief summary. I said that this was something that had been in the works for about a year. I told them that I knew the risks, that Robin and I had done our homework and prayed about it, and that we really felt good about it. I started to get emotional, and I said that this was supposed to happen, and that we were grateful to be presented with this opportunity.

Now I'm in my bed and it's almost midnight. I'm just crying. I feel so close to this. I am prepared. All these battles I have been fighting in order to have this opportunity are molding me and making me stronger. Stronger for what? Just to donate? I don't think so. There is more out there. Experiences and understanding lead to more, and I have more coming. Perhaps this is one of the reasons I have kept a journal. I can look back and see what it took. The challenges, the fun, the relationships, and on and on. I am a seeker of experiences, and this is a major one.

June 25, 2018

Oh Doctor! - Jerry Coleman

This afternoon, I had a follow up visit with Dr. Jellyfinger. He reevaluated the full press plan and decided everything was going according to plan and that I was on my way to the table. BAM!

Jellyfinger also said he was happy to help and that he was glad my illness happened when it did because he was leaving tomorrow for a two-week vacation. What!? Wait a minute here! I think we need to add this to our scorecard. I am not a doctor guy. I don't go to the doctor. I just don't go. I'm not even a once-a-year-go-in-for-your-annual-physical guy. And yet, I had emailed my doctor and practically told him to tell me to chill and wait it out.

Instead, Nurse Goodtidings got me an appointment that day and Jellyfinger discovered my asthma and implemented the full court press to get me back in the game! Dr. Jellyfinger should be named Dr. Thorough because he is just that! How many doctors would have just told me to let nature run its course? How many would have missed the asthma? And I just happened to come in right before his two-week vacation. Just another coincidence? I think not!

June 27, 2018

Here I Go Again - White Snake

Today is Wednesday. Surgery is next Tuesday. The countdown is on. Well, it's been on for a while, really. I know I said I was done with tests and labs and all that, and I truly thought I was. But apparently, they do a last-minute lab workup just to make sure you're still healthy and ready to go. I have actually been looking forward to this. I have no idea why. I don't really enjoy it, but I have been looking forward to this one last suckout of my veins. Robin tells me they will be sticking, poking, and prodding when I have the surgery. I guess I am used to it. Doesn't sound convincing, but I should be used to it.

Yesterday afternoon, I could not remember if I was supposed to be fasting for these labs. I looked through the emails and found no directions. I assumed that because nothing I read said I was supposed to fast and nobody told me to, that I did not need to. However, I had to fast for most of the labs I have taken, and I wanted to make sure. I called Nurse Nightingale yesterday afternoon and got her voicemail.

Nightingale's voicemail said she would be out of the office and on vacation this week! Huh? That's funny. During our conversation five days ago, she told me to call anytime for anything. She made me feel all warm inside, and then she went on vacation? Why didn't she tell me she was going on vacation? I know people need vacations, but why didn't she tell me she was going to be gone next week instead of telling me to call her if I had any questions? She knew she was going on vacation, right? And it was the week before my operation. Come on, Nightingale. Then I called and left messages for Nurse Teresa and Nurse Downer. Those were all the numbers I had.

This morning at 7:45 AM, I took my last and final labs after fasting. When in doubt, error on the side of fasting. Regrettably, Mr. Stick was not there, but the other tech did a fine job. He spilled out the vials onto the metal cookie sheet as gracefully as Stick. I took a picture of the giant rack filled with vials of my blood and sent it to Steve. He texted me back that Jenny was doing the same thing. Kind of cool to think we were taking our last labs at the same time. Then he texted that he was wondering what was going to go wrong next. NOTHING! Let's rock and roll!

June 29, 2018: Morning

You Spin Me Round - Dead or Alive

YOU ARE NEVER GONNA BELIEVE THIS! It's Friday. Robin and I are flying to Utah on Monday. Surgery is Tuesday. I got a call from Nurse Downer at 3:45 PM. She said my labs show elevated levels and I need to retake them. They need to see if they really are high. Seriously?! Can't they give me a pass just this once? They know I'm going to pass the next round. That's what I do! I fail and then I pass, EVERY STINKING TIME! It's cyclical. I fail then pass, fail then pass. It spins like a record baby right round, round, round!

She asked when we were arriving in Utah. I told her late Monday morning. She said that would be too late to get labs done there. I have a thousand things to get done today before we leave, and then I miss two weeks of work and life. I don't need this today! Shoot! I don't need this at all! But I told her I would do it here today. I was downtown working and emailed Dr. Jellyfinger about the crisis. I got the auto reply that he was out of town.

I knew he was gone, but I was hoping that Nurse Goodtidings would intercept the email and save the day. I called the Sharp lab, and they told me to come in. I bolted to the lab while Nurse Downer sent in my lab orders.

Apparently, I am out, AGAIN! Even after being approved by the board! I have to pass these labs. If I don't, then everything was for naught! I am sooo freakin' tired of this song. The logistics are tricky. The Transplant Center sent the orders to my lab, and I am on the way there now. I called and they are expecting me. The only problem is that there was a huge accident on Interstate 5 North and traffic is at a standstill! How many exclamation points am I going to use today!? Not joking, traffic is maddening!

June 29, 2018: Afternoon

Fight For Your Right - Beastie Boys

I went from downtown to Del Mar using side streets most of the way. I had to get to the lab before they closed, and I did. At 4:45, with 15 minutes to spare. I walked in and nobody was there. It was a ghost town. Looked like nobody made it to their appointments and people did not show up for work because of the massive accident and/or people went home early because the freeway was closed.

Luckily, there was one guy there. (There was also someone in the back who I did not see until later.) For some reason, the lab tech I was dealing with saw my order but could not process it. It was the same thing I had gone through every time I came in with orders from outside of their network. The problem this time was that the person in the office who verifies the orders was not there! Somebody needed to approve them, but nobody was there.

I said "They're in the system. This is the third or fourth time I've come in with lab orders from the University of Utah and they were approved every time. You can look it up. I am the most popular customer in this lab. I know everyone here except you." He told me he was new and was the only guy there at the moment. He was understanding, but said that every time I was here before, the "business people" were there, and they were the ones that needed to approve everything, and right then, they weren't there.

He kept telling me, "I can't do it...I cannot process this order... I can't do it. It's the protocol... I will get in trouble." Then he turned around and walked into a back room like he was doing something. He expected me to leave, but obviously, he did not know who he was dealing with. I kept talking. I was really nice about it. I used all my best people skills on the new guy. Then he said, "You want me to call my superior?" I said, "Yeah. Call your superior." He called and I could hear his side of the conversation. At one point, I heard him say, "I need somebody to tell this guy that I can't do it." I was tired and so done with this game and, when he got off the phone, things between us got a little heated:

Me: Look, I am giving a kidney on Tuesday. I was here two days ago, and my labs were elevated. So, I need to take them again. We need to figure this out because there are plane tickets involved. There is money and time on the line, and there is a woman whose life is hanging in the balance."

New Guy: Look, I'm trying to do everything I can.

Me: No, you're not. I just heard you say on the phone that you needed someone to tell this guy that you can't do anything. You're not trying to find solutions. You're just trying to cover your butt and get rid of me.

My good people skills were gone, and now I was getting mad. New Guy was getting mad too, but I was not going anywhere, and he had to be there, so the standoff ensued. Then I remembered one time when I got the labs approved and the "business people" were not there. That time, Nurse Goodtidings had come out of nowhere to save the day.

Me: My doctor's office is next door. I'll go over there and see if we can get him to approve it.

New Guy: Sounds good. If he approves, then we're good to go.

I walked next door and the office was dark. It was not just Jellyfinger's office; all the offices were dark. There was nobody around. Interstate 5, which is a main artery and is right outside the door to the office, had shut everything down. I went back to the lab.

Me: It's dark. There's no one around. But can someone go back there? Someone could be back there. Dr. Jellyfinger is on vacation, but someone is filling in for him and Nurse Goodtidings could be back there. Anyone could be there having coffee or doing something.

By this time, the person in the back of the lab was interacting with us. She said that she would take a look and see if she could find someone. In the meantime, New Guy had found new strength. All of a sudden, he was calling everybody and doing everything he could do.

New Guy: Okay, I got three things going on to get this approved. I called my boss back. He is actually the guy who took your labs on Wednesday, and he does remember you. He is helping me out.

I remembered that guy and he was super cool, so I knew he was banging on doors for me. I could really tell that everyone was trying to figure this out. I apologized for being a jerk. New Guy said, "No, no, no, no. I'm sorry. I could have handled this better. So, we're all sorry. It's all good." I said, "Look, you're just doing what you gotta do and I'm doing what I gotta do."

It was past 5:00 PM now. The few people who were in the building were walking out the door. I could tell New Guy's day was done, but he wasn't going anywhere. He was really trying to help me out and that was pretty awesome. The girl working with him, who went next door and could not find anyone, was leaving. She was done. But not New Guy. He's my brother now. He was on the phone executing all the plans. Exploring every avenue.

Two women in scrubs came walking by and I asked, "Either of you a doctor?" They were nurses, but they were cool. It's like every single time, everything I do, there's a battle for everything. Someone on the other side is always testing me, asking me, how bad do I want it? I looked at the clock and it said 5:20. I had now kept New Guy at work 20 minutes late on a day when most of his coworkers and people in the building bailed early to get their weekend on. Then New Guy came out.

New Guy: We just got an in-house doctor to approve it.

Me: We're gonna do it?!

New Guy: Yeah, we're doing it.

Me: Unbelievable.

I walked back into the lab and who walked up? Seriously, who walked up at this moment?! Time stood still. It was like that moment in X-Men when that guy with super speed saves everyone. The picture froze and he's walking around moving people. That is what it was like when Nurse Goodtidings walked in.

I knew instantly that she was the "doctor" who approved the labs. I don't know where she was or how she did it, but she did it again! She walked up and said, "Hi, you're approved." I announced to the empty lobby, "Ladies and gentleman, Nurse Goodtidings coming through in the clutch yet again!" I thanked her profusely. Amazing. First, she approved my labs in a nearly identical situation just before Christmas and then she got me those labs by the skin of my teeth just before the extended Christmas weekend. And now, she comes through again. Unreal.

I went back to the lab sticking room and got stuck for the last time. I keep saying that, don't I? Well, I am pretty sure this is the last time. We fly out on Monday, so the next time a needle gets inserted into my flesh will be in Utah. My labs won't be ready until Monday morning. Everyone knows that time is of the essence, so I hope we get them before we fly out.

June 30, 2018

I Ain't Worried - OneRepublic

Ever feel like you just can't get it all done? Well, today was filled with getting all the work done that should have been done yesterday, and the day before, and so on. And yet, I'm leaving Monday morning. What doesn't get done today will have to wait a couple weeks; I am going to spend Sunday with my family.

The Petersens' congregation is fasting again. Here is the reminder email that they should begin their fast today:

Subject: Reminder: Ward Fast this Sunday

Brothers and Sister of the Farmington Ranches 4th Ward,

As was announced Sunday, the Ward Council has asked that we hold a Ward fast on Sister Jenny Petersen's behalf. The opportunity we have to put our own needs and wants aside to provide this service to our Ward family is a blessing. I would encourage each of you to prepare yourselves for this fast by praying for Sister Petersen and include prayers for Brother Rick Daynes who is selflessly donating his kidney to Sister Petersen.

We have been asked to focus on two key areas as we pray and fast:

1. That Rick Daynes (kidney donor) will make it through the kidney transplant without complication, that he will recover quickly and completely, that the longevity and overall health of his life won't be impacted adversely, and that Rick and his family will be blessed for Rick's extraordinary act of kindness.

2. That Jenny will make it through the kidney transplant without complication, and that her body will receive the new kidney without rejection, and that it will perform optimally and for the maximum duration.

We want to add our testimony that there is power in prayer and fasting, as we supplicate the Lord on behalf of these two wonderful children of our Heavenly Father, He will pour out His blessings.

The Ward Council and the Petersen family would like to thank you in advance for your love and support during this difficult time.

Love,

The Bishopric,

It's humbling to think of so many good people praying and fasting for us. The men in my congregation have also been invited to join in this fast, as well as my family. I shot off the following email.

Sat 6/30/2018 10:52 AM

Dear Family,

There are a lot of people fasting for the Petersens and Daynes today and tomorrow. You are invited to join in. Jenny's health has been in decline for a long time and we are hoping, praying, fasting, that a Daynes kidney will not just save her life, but restore health, strength, and energy so she can go on doing what she does. Jenny is a young mother of four great kids. Her number one, Jon, just turned 16 last week. Jon has Down Syndrome and needs his mom to be around for a long time. If you could add longevity in your prayers, that would be sweet. And if you think about it, a good recovery for me would be cool.

Thanks,

Rick

As busy as I am today, my number one priority is of course, prepping for donation. Who knows what will happen to the labs and if they will get to the U? Yesterday, among the craziness of getting my last labs done, Nurse Goodtidings told me she was leaving on vacation as well. She's my go to, my rock, my problem solver, my rescuer. I was in a bit of a panic. Goodtidings explained that she had left a detailed message to the nurse taking her place. I have the fill-in's email and phone number and, apparently, she knows exactly what to do. We'll see.

Covering all loose ends, I shot off the following emails to everyone involved in getting my labs to the Transplant Center Monday morning.

From: Rick Daynes
To: Nurse Downer
Date: Sat 6/30/2018 12:36 PM
Subject: Re: lab order

Hi Downer,

By some small miracle, I completed the labs Friday evening. Long story short, I had to get my doctor to order them. He will have the results Monday morning and will forward them to your email. His nurse is Proxy and she will be the one forwarding. Nurse Proxy also has your phone number. My doctor is Dr. Jellyfinger of Sharp Rees Stealey here in San Diego. His office is the Del Mar office. I don't have a number.

My wife and I depart at 10:00 AM and arrive in SLC at 1:00. Please stay in touch. We can go to the U when we land, if necessary.

Thanks,

Rick Daynes

From: Rick Daynes
To: Nurse Proxy
Date: 06/30/2018 12:28 pm
Subject: THIS IS THE MESSAGE YOU HAVE BEEN WAITING FOR!

Hi Proxy, this is Rick Daynes. Monday morning, the labs that I did on Friday (not Wednesday) should be in Dr. Jellyfinger's inbox. Please forward those results to

Downer.Downer@hsc.utah.edu Her phone number is
555-123-4567. Also please forward the results to me.

Thank you!

Rick

July 1, 2018

Celebration - Kool and the Gang

Today was rad. I love Sundays anyway, but today was
extra cool. First off, my family was all home, which
was nice. There was a pretty large fast going on and
a lot of families and many friends were involved. The
Petersens' entire ward congregation in Farmington,
Utah: all fasting. They had a "break the fast," in which
they invited Ozz (my brother) to say the prayer.

That's kind of cool. My brother got to represent not
just me, but our entire family. Hundreds of people
prayed and fasted for Jenny, the Petersens, me, and
the rest of the Daynes. It's humbling, to say the least.

This evening, Robin went to the airport to pick up
Julie Miller. Julie is Jenny's sister and will be taking
care of our kids for the first half of the week. Jenny's
sister-in-law will be flying in mid-week and taking care
of our kids for the second half. It's all part of the deal
Steve and I negotiated. He offered free babysitting for
an entire week, so Robin and I could have a Parents
Only Getaway (POG). I countered with a kidney.

Robin said that, when she and Julie met, Julie was
already crying. That's just really sweet. I met her

when they arrived home. She gave me a hug and thanked me. It was a touching moment. Then we introduced her to our kids, laid the groundwork for the week, and went to bed.

July 2, 2018: Morning

I'm Leaving on a Jet Plane - John Denver

I was checking my phone for calls, emails, and texts, and looking at my hospital app from the moment I woke up this morning. I needed those lab results from Friday ASAP. Goodtidings told me Friday that she was going on vacation. Yes, that's correct. Three major players on my healthcare team were on vacation. Nurse Nightingale, Dr. Jellyfinger, and Nurse Goodtidings all decided to take vacay this week. Is there a medical conference going on somewhere? (Note to self: Next time I donate a kidney, make sure my medical team is going to stick around.)

Nurse Teresa was back from her trip to the Bahamas, but I hadn't heard much from her. You know when you go on vacation, and everyone throws stuff on your plate for you to take care of when you get home? That's probably why I haven't heard from Teresa.

Nurse Goodtidings gave me great instructions, though. She said Nurse Proxy, who was taking her place, would check for the labs and that she knew exactly what to do when they came in. I had sent Nurse Proxy an email on Friday just to establish contact and to make sure she knew all the contact info and where to send the reports. In the subject line,

I wrote, "Proxy! THIS IS THE MESSAGE YOU HAVE BEEN WAITING FOR!" Think she knew it was me?

The morning was filled with packing, checking for lab results on my online account, making sure the kids were good, checking for lab results, double checking rides and plans, checking for lab results, packing, etc. I finally got tired of checking my email and online account and started making calls. That did not help, until…

On the way to the airport, I reached a random person at my doctor's office. Yes, Dr. Jellyfinger and Nurse Goodtidings were gone, but Proxy had been briefed and knew what to do. Unfortunately, she wasn't in. The first thing I asked the woman on the phone was, were my lab results in? She looked and told me no, they weren't there. No results, no nothing. I thanked her and I told her that those lab results were a huge deal, so I would be calling back and I hope she didn't mind. She said that would be fine and we hung up.

After getting to our gate at the airport, I called the doctor's office again. Same woman. She told me the results still weren't there. Then she looked in a different place and found them! Bam! Results were in! I asked her to email them to me. She said she could not do that. She was not allowed to email them to anyone. I said, why not? They are my results. She told me to check my account page online, and they would be there. I told her I was looking at my account page at that exact moment and they were not there.

I asked her to fax them to the University of Utah. You guessed it! She could not do that either. What!? She wouldn't email them to me, the results weren't on my account page with the hospital, and she would not fax them to the Transplant Center that gave the initial lab order. Then it dawned on me. Maybe she won't send them because it was "Dr." Nurse Goodtidings who approved the order. Stupid HIPAA!

At this point, Robin and I were literally about to step onto a plane for Salt Lake City. Those results would tell me if I should even be getting on the plane, and this woman wouldn't budge.

Me: You need to talk to Proxy, can you talk to Proxy?

Woman: Who is Proxy?

Me: She is Goodtidings sub today.

Woman: Let me see.

I was on hold for a few seconds when an 801 number called in. I switched over of course, because all 801 numbers were top priority. It was the Transplant Clinic, but it was someone I had never spoken to. The woman said she was calling to do my pre-check in for tomorrow. I said, "Can I call you back? I have a few things I gotta get done or I won't be checking in at all tomorrow." I asked her if she could get word to Nurse Downer or whoever was covering for Nurse Nightingale that my lab results were in and I was doing everything I could to get them to the hospital ASAP. I said this all in one breath because I was in a serious rush. Poor girl just called to ask me a couple questions. I could hear the surprise in her voice as she said, "Oh, oh yes, I'll do that."

I clicked back over to my doctor's office. I was pretty sure she had hung up.

Me: Hello? Hello?

Voice: Hi, this is Proxy.

Me: REALLY!

Proxy: Yes really! Is this Rick?

Me: Yes, and I am so excited to talk to you!

Proxy: Hey, guy! I got your email and all the instructions from Goodtidings. I'm gonna fax these lab results right over to the University of Utah.

Me: YEAH BABY! Thank you so much!

Proxy: You are welcome, and you call me back if you need anything else.

We hung up as the final boarding call echoed through the terminal and we were on our way. I called Nurse Downer as we walked in line through the floating walkway and told her my lab results should be coming through the fax machine now. She said she'd check and call me back.

Then my phone rang with some random work questions and just like that, I was that guy. You know that guy on the phone, on the passenger boarding bridge, walking in line, moving down the aisle, and then in his seat, on his cell the entire time? That guy bugs me. And now, that's me, and I'm bugging myself! The flight attendants were getting ready to shut the doors so we could taxi, and my phone was blowing up with email and texts regarding lab results and finding people and last-minute this and thats. I snuck in one more call to Downer:

167

Nurse Downer: We did get your results. I am holding them right now.

Me: YES! Okay, and what do they say?

Nurse Downer: Hmmm, ummm (waffling), I cannot tell.

Me: You can tell me, they're my results.

Nurse Downer: No, I mean I am not sure what these results mean. They are better, but not sure it's where we want you to be.

Me: Can you just give me the go ahead? That's all I need.

Nurse Downer: I cannot do that. Everybody has to weigh in. Everybody has to give their opinion.

Me: Are you talking about the board? The board that approved me? They all have to see these new results and weigh in?

Nurse Downer: Yes.

Me: I am on a fully loaded plane right now and the doors are shutting. If I will not be on the operating table tomorrow, you need to say something now.

Nurse Downer: Just come, I should have a definite answer for you when your flight gets here.

I hung up and caught a couple stink eyes from fellow passengers, letting me know that cell phones should have been turned off and stowed long ago. Again, I was now that guy. It was good to have my wife with me at this moment. The anxiety was palpable and the strangers around us could feel it. There we sat with the plane taxiing, then turning, and taking off, and we were unsure of what would happen in the next two hours while we were airborne and out of communication.

It's hard to believe all the build up to this event and I still did not have the green light. We could land and the board could still say no. Jenny Petersen, tomorrow's recipient of my kidney, would be picking us up from the airport. How cruel would it be to land and then find out the operation was canceled? To find out that they were putting a stop to this the day before the operation and moments before jumping into the car with my recipient? Or worse, what if they called me when we were together and delivered the bad news?

I don't think that will happen though. We have come too far to stop now. The surgery is tomorrow, for crying out loud! By this time tomorrow, it will be done.

July 2, 2018: Afternoon

Hold On - Wilson Phillips

When the plane landed, I booted up my phone. Yes, it was well before the flight attendant announced we could turn on electronic devices. I was still that guy. There were emails from all the major players in today's saga regarding everything faxed, emailed, received, and pending approval. What was missing was anything letting me know that I was approved and that all systems were go for tomorrow.

169

Robin and I walked through the airport, grabbed some bags and met Jenny. It was good to see her, and we chatted about all the family preparations leading up to tomorrow. Between our two families, there are nine kids, some with special needs, and a lot of plans to be orchestrated.

Jenny drove us to pick up a rental car, and I was really uneasy. Robin and I were not going to say a thing about this morning's recent lab results. No way we were bringing that up. At the car rental, I snuck away and recorded some thoughts on my cell.

My recording: "We are with Jenny, my recipient, and it's great being here, but unsettling at the same time. Because we're still not cleared for surgery. It is tomorrow. We are here, and not cleared. Not a chance we are going to tell Jenny. No way. Stressful."

Robin and I jumped in the rental and drove to our next meeting place, lunch with Steve and Jenny at our favorite SLC restaurant, The Red Iguana. There we were, talking about tomorrow and enjoying our meal. There was a buzz of excitement in the air. Everyone was in good spirits. We talked about Jenny's sister, who was currently taking care of our kids. We talked about the Petersens and all their prep for the big day, as well as the recovery. There was much to be done. Then they asked me how I was doing. I thought, well I haven't been cleared yet, but other than that, everything's fine.

The talking and eating continued while, inside, I was fretting. I got a call from the Transplant Center and let it go to voicemail. I was going to sneak away from the table after the voicemail popped up. However, the caller did not leave a voicemail. Lunch ended and

Robin and I went to our rental. At this point, we were clear of the Petersens, so I checked my email. There was something from Nurse Downer.

She wrote the words I had been waiting to hear all day. Actually, I had been waiting to hear these words for a few days now: "You're good to go. You're cleared and good to go for tomorrow." Relief finally set in. I reclined my seat. The day was warm, and the sun was shining as we both relaxed and let the stress melt away. It was finally over. Truly over. No more tests. No more board meetings to approve or disapprove my case. No more emails or calls telling me to do something again. No more sticks or peeing in cups or evaluations. Final approval given. We were good and I felt so much better.

Nurse Downer called while we were on the way to my brother's house just to make sure I got the message. She said, "Yeah. So, I had to get everyone's opinion. Everyone's got an opinion. And you're cleared and ready to go."

I then called the pre-check woman back. Remember her? The woman who called this morning when we were boarding a flight in San Diego? I answered all the questions and officially passed my pre-check screening. Got another call from the Transplant Center. This time it was the surgery scheduling people. We got lucky and have the later of the two surgeries tomorrow. Check-in time, 9:00 AM. Stoked.

July 2, 2018: Evening

I Gotta Feeling - Black Eyed Peas

Robin and I went to Ozz and Lindsay's and had a good time hanging with them. The Petersens came over and we ate pizza and salad on the back lawn and sat around and talked.

By and by, I did get around to telling them we had another snafoo in our quest, and we were not cleared until two hours ago. It's done right? We were checking into the hospital in the morning. No sense in holding anything back. This was the time to be grateful and laugh and shake our heads a bit.

I started the story by saying, "So in keeping with our theme of this whole experience, I again failed or was in some gray area with my last labs and had to take them again. I did this by the skin of my teeth on Friday and got the results just as we stepped on the plane this morning. Long story short, the board had to weigh in again and I finally got cleared to donate after lunch, at the 11th hour, in the Red Iguana parking lot. Their reaction was predictable.

Jenny shook her head and Steve laughed. They couldn't believe it. Then it got even better because I told them the story of getting a cold and finding out my cold triggered my childhood asthma that I did not know I had. And how Dr. Jellyfinger instituted a full court press to get me healthy. Also, how I was supposed to be backpacking through the High Sierra mountains and blah, blah, blah, all of the unbelievable things that had happened recently.

I was cool because my nieces and nephew as well as the Petersen kids were all there. It was a pretty good lesson about who was in charge.

Time After Time - Cindy Lauper

Then it was the Petersens' turn to entertain. And by the Petersens, I don't mean Steve. NO, you would think that, but not this time. Jenny started talking and you could tell she had a little something prepared. She talked about her faith in the Lord Jesus Christ. She said she knew that no matter what happened, families are forever, and she was very secure in that. She gave Lindsey and Ozz a framed picture of Christ and then gave us the same gift. She said this picture of Christ really hit her and she spoke about the features that made it so appealing. She then gave me and Robin a bag of Lifesavers candies because, she said, I was her lifesaver.

She had one more gift to give and she handed me a box. She talked about time and how precious it is. She said that ever since she got sick, she felt like there was a clock ticking on her life. I opened the box and pulled out a beautiful wooden clock. I loved it right away.

Then I discovered an engraving on the clock: "Thank you for the immeasurable gift of time." Jenny said that she just wanted to be a mom and that she could not have been more gracious or thankful about my gift. She said, "You know, we can never repay you for this gift." There were tears and laughter and sweet somber moments. She gave us a very sweet card:

Dear Rick and Robin, can you believe this day has come? We still look back at all the miracles that have unfolded throughout this trial over the last three years, and there are simply no words to adequately describe our gratitude to you. You are the miracle that seemed almost impossible for so long. You are the reason I have hope. My greatest desire is to have the opportunity to be a wife and mother a little longer. And you are giving me that chance. Your unselfish act is truly remarkable, and we hope you continue to be richly blessed for it. We love you. Stephen and Jenny.

After reading that, we were all a mess. We said goodbye and stopped at Cherry Berry on our way out of there for some frozen yogurt. We drove to Draper, where we checked into Uncle Rob and Aunt Connie's house, unpacked, and hit the hay.

PART 2
DONATION

July 3, 2018

Today's the Day - Mel Fisher

7:20 AM It's the day before our nation's Independence Day, which is a momentous day for our family and others for additional reasons. It is the morning of the Big Day. It feels surreal and I cannot believe we are finally here. I didn't sleep very well at all, but I feel good.

But, you know, I've never given a kidney before and it's a little unsettling knowing that I'll be going under the knife. Or maybe we'll show up and someone has pulled the plug on this operation again. I do have faith and no doubt everything will work out for the best for everyone involved. I've donned my Mel Fisher's "Today's the Day" tee shirt, a shirt I save for occasions like today. Because today truly is the day.

8:46 AM OK. It's almost 9:00. Robin and I are set for a 9:00 AM check-in time. I just wanted to record this moment. My pre-game plan was to go early to the University of Utah and drive over to Red Butte Gardens, which is one of my favorite places in Salt Lake. I thought it would be the perfect place to relax and reflect prior to check-in. It has been years since I have been there and now there are museums next to the gardens and apparently you now have to pay an admission fee to get in. COME ON PEOPLE! I gotta pay to get into the park? I would actually pay, but they are NOT OPEN!

Not good University of Utah! I'm about to give an organ and I am denied admittance to my favorite park? Do people not like to hit the park before 9:00 in the morning on a summer's day? My pre-game has taken a hit. Rant over.

We're just hangin' at the museum, walking around, poking our heads in the windows. It feels good to be with my wife, holding hands, and being in the moment. The air is dry with a morning chill and we are quite comfortable in shorts and sweatshirts. We're good. I'm at peace.

We have had so many sweet moments in our lives. This is one of those times. One of the reasons we go on POGs is because we create and remind each other of how many sweet moments we have. This will be one of those times we will always remember and cherish. This is what we do and it's rad.

I love my wife and she is absolutely enamored with me. It's gonna be a great day.

Cuts Like a Knife and it Feels So Right - Bryan Adams

The following entry was recorded on July 5th at 5:02 AM. It recaps the two previous days (July 3–4) beginning where Robin and I left off at Red Butte Gardens.

Following a hand-holding stroll and a reflection in the parking lot and on a bench at the entrance to Red

Butte Gardens, Robin and I drove the short distance to the University of Utah Medical Center and checked in at exactly 8:59 AM. I have nothing but positive things to say about this hospital. It is a great facility with good people. Steve and I had been texting back and forth through the morning with our usual sarcasm.

Steve: You gonna make it today?

Me: Shoot! Was that today?

Steve: We're all checked in.

Me: I'll stop by if I'm in the area. We're gonna make a stop and pick up some Blistex for you. Worried you won't have enough.

Steve: It's the first thing I packed. Got plenty.

Robin and I went up to the third floor and checking in was easy like Sunday Morning. We met up with the Petersens and walked out onto the terrace and took pictures and mingled for a few minutes. The sun was shining and just beginning to warm up the benches of the Salt Lake Valley. The wind was a whisper and smiles were all around.

It felt great to be there. Jenny looked happy and ready to go. I could not detect any nervousness in her although I am sure it was there. The conversation was light, spirits were high, and everyone was calm. Or at least everyone seemed calm. We went back into the lobby and said, "see you soon" to the Petersens as they were ushered to their room and Robin and I to ours.

We signed even more forms and gowned up. Will they ever find a better option than the standard hospital gown? Seriously, trillions of dollars are spent continuously upgrading medicine and medical equipment, yet the archaic, open-back hospital gown your grandmother wore is still the go-to dresswear of the ultra-modern hospital. That actually gives me a great idea for my next party theme.

More nurses came and went, prepping us for the day. Dr. Harvest popped in to say hi. I asked him if he could record the operation. He said he probably could have if I had requested sooner. Dang! Why didn't I think of that sooner? He did say he would take a picture of my kidney, which I thought was cool.

The anesthesiologist came in. He looked like he was 16 years old. I was tempted to ask if he had his driver's license or if his mommy gave him a ride to work. But Robin beat me to the punch with a far less insulting question about the type of drugs I would be receiving. The anesthesiologist did acknowledge his youthful appearance and told us he gets comments about it all the time.

The nurses inserted the IV and we discussed the timeline for the rest of the day. It's interesting, right? How long does it take to extract a kidney? What do they do with it once it's in hand or bowl or the little ice chest with the red cross symbol on the outside? At what point do they open the recipient? What kind of prep work is done there?

We learned that Jenny would be going in about half an hour after me. I have my own team anchored by none other than Doctor Harvest. At some point during the operation, Harvest signals the transplant team anchored by Doctor Sew, and they get to work.

At about 11:00 AM, I began to make off-color remarks about myself, others, and my surroundings. Robin said, "looks like the drugs are working," which was a surprise to me. I knew the IV was in, but I did not know the drugs were flowing. Doogie Howser, the anesthesiologist, wheeled me out of my room and into the hall where I thought Steve shook my hand and Robin kissed me. Now half baked, I wanted to make sure, so I asked, "who kissed me?" To which Robin replied, "Did it taste like Blistex?"

Dr. Doogie then wheeled me into the operating room, which was way bigger than I imagined. But then again, I was stoned and slipping into la la land. I saw the team assembled and ready to cut me open, but I did not see Dr. Harvest. I fought the Zs and told everyone I did not want to go under until I saw Dr. Harvest. It was important for me to see him there in the operating room. You never know in these situations. What if they ran a bait and switch? What if something happened to him in the last hour and he wasn't feeling up to it today? Who is in the bullpen? Does Doogie scrub in?

I heard a member of the team announce the arrival of the chief surgeon and point him out on the other side of the room. He was all suited up and waved to me. I said, "glad to see you came to work today." Which did not make sense of course because I had already seen him, but you say stupid things when you're high as a kite. I remember putting my head straight, looking up, and announcing, "Let's do this thing." Then I was out.

Sweet Dreams are Made of This - Eurythmics

The following entry was delivered verbally to me from Robin and Steve. I did have to speculate a bit while piecing things together and the timing might not be completely accurate. You know, cause I was busy dreaming

Almost an hour after Dr. Doogie wheeled me away from my wife and I'm guessing 50 minutes into the operation, Robin got a call from one of the nurses. She told my wife that I was doing fine and that everything was going well. She said she would call back in about two hours, around 2:00 PM.

About 1:20 PM, Robin got a text from Steve saying that they had yet to take Jenny back. This is where things become a little unclear and tense. The Petersens had been told that they would take Jenny back about 30 minutes after me, so that would have been around 11:30. They also knew that Jenny would not be opened until the kidney was out.

Robin said that at this point she kind of began to worry and freak out a bit. She texted Steve, "That's way longer than they told us." She shed a tear as thoughts crept into her head about why this was taking so long. Jenny, the kidney recipient, was almost two hours late being wheeled into the operating room. What could possibly be the reason?

Robin was alone. I was in surgery having a major organ extracted. The process is complicated. Whereas they used to enter via the back or the side, close to where the kidney lives, they now enter the front. There are three insertions. Two are mainly for instruments and cameras. The main cut goes from the belly button down and this is where the kidney comes out.

Like a Surgeon - Weird Al Yanchovic

Doctors switched from side/back extraction and began extracting the kidney from the front when they realized it made recovery easier for the patient. Here's how it works: Once that incision in the belly is made, there is an obstacle course to navigate to get to the kidneys at the back. Guts have to be moved, unstuck, and worked with so a kidney from the stern can exit. Once the kidney and pathway have been established, there is a web of flesh and blood and fat to cut, cap, fuse, and solder in order to free the organ.

When that is done, the surgeon inserts his hand through the patient's belly and down the pathway to the organ. He then grabs the kidney with his hand and pulls it out of the body. Then he hoists the pulsating kidney in one hand over his head and screams out, "EUREKA!" Okay, that last part might not be true, but the surgeon does extract the kidney with his own hand. I'd yell eureka or shazam or something if I was able to get a kidney safely out of another human.

Back to Robin. With all that in mind, and thinking they were almost two hours late in bringing in the kidney recipient, she was CONCERNED. I cannot imagine where her mind and anxiety were headed. The surgery is pretty safe, but that is quite a journey from the belly button to the kidneys with a lot of vital parts in between.

Even for a calm, registered nurse, it was impossible not to worry and question what the heck was going on. The nervousness lasted another 20 minutes until Steve appeared and said they had wheeled Jenny back for part two of the transplant. At this point, Robin regained her composure and figured the kidney was almost out.

15 minutes later, around 2:00 PM, Dr. Harvest appeared to announce that my surgery went smoothly. The kidney was out, and he had a great picture of it (at that point, still very much in my body). He showed Robin and Steve. There was a lot of fat around my kidney, which everyone, including me, was surprised to see. Doc said they had to trim the fat to get that kidney out.

The picture itself is pretty surreal. First, it is amazing to think that Harvest had a camera good enough to take this shot. Second, it's rad to think that my kidney, which had been working in my body all my life, had gone to a new home to provide the same function for someone else. Dr. Harvest said it was a big, beefy, kidney with lots of fat around it. He talked about the nice, long arteries and veins and said that it was simply perfect. He said, "Rick was made to donate...His body was made to give that kidney."

Dr. Harvest told Steve and Robin that I would be wheeled into the recovery room in about an hour. I guess that once the kidney is extracted, Dr. Harvest is out of there. I mean, it was his second surgery of the day, and he does have a team with him. I'm guessing he hands the kidney off to someone who cuts more fat and prepares it for a new home. I am also guessing he leaves the next surgeon in line to move everything back to its original place, sew me up, and clean up the mess.

About 3:00 PM, which was the time Dr. Harvest told Robin I would be done, I was still nowhere to be seen. 3:30 PM came and went. At almost 4:00 PM, I still wasn't out. Around this time, Steve got a call from Dr. Sew's team that Jenny was now being opened up. Robin and Steve were beside themselves thinking the kidney had been on ice this whole time. Or did it take this long to trim it up and get it ready? We all assumed the surgeries, and especially the insertion of the kidney, would go a lot quicker than it was.

About 4:00, Robin got the room number where we would be for the next couple days and headed up there. She texted Steve and my brother Ozz about me and Jenny and where we might be and when we might go to the rooms. After all was said and done, we believe my actual surgery was between two and three hours. I went to the post-op area for a while. There was some shuffling of the recovery rooms, no doubt to give me a room with a view. Actually, we did request a room overlooking the valley so we could see fireworks tomorrow night. That could have factored into the delay.

As Robin set up camp in our recovery room, the nurses told her I would be there in about 20 minutes. Well, 20 minutes came and went. And then another and another and so on. Steve and Ozz kept texting Robin, asking if she had seen me yet. She figured it was a logistical hold-up, but again her mind wondered if there had been a problem somewhere. Eventually, the nurses started asking questions and somebody called to see what the hold-up was.

A game of he-said, she-said was in play and I, shoot, I was out like a light. I could have been on the roof, for all I knew. Around 6:00 PM, I finally arrived in my room and was reunited with my wife. Robin thinks Jenny made it to her room before I made it to mine. Ozz and Lindsey had already been there for an hour and came to the room. I was seeing visitors in my sleep. They took selfies with me while I was out cold.

Everyone was about to leave when I woke up. I remember being extremely groggy, but happy to see my sweet wife. I was also happy to see Ozz and Lindsey there. We have this funny ritual in our family whenever someone is running a distance race, in a big sporting event, or sick. Basically, whenever anyone needs some energy, we clasp hands and pretend energy is transferring from one person to another. I told Ozz I needed an energy transfer, which we did, but it only made me more tired.

Pop Goes the Weasel - Barney

We visited for a while, and when I say we, I mean Robin, Ozz, and Lindsey. I was in and out of consciousness. My wife, Robin, was now Nurse Robin with a patient to care for. Even though she had visitors, she wasted no time in assessing the patient and his wounds.

She undressed me to the point of seeing the three incisions on my belly and THERE IT WAS! Not my stitches. Not the purple bruising or massive swelling. Something was sticking out like a sore thumb and shouting for attention. I don't even know how to describe it. My once perfect innie belly button was now stretched to maximum capacity and was sticking straight out. It was like there was an animal in there, trying to escape. My belly was swelling and nothing was stopping the fluid from popping that belly button straight out.

At 6:14 PM, Steve sent us a picture of Jenny's catheter bag. Steve said it was draining like crazy and that a liter and a half had filled up over the last 30 to 40 minutes. We also received some drawings the Petersen kids made of the kidney. They actually named it. My kidney or now Jenny's kidney had a name. Felix. I liked it. From then on, when referring to the kidney, we simply said Felix. It had a name, a life, a personality.

Felix was working overtime, filtering and draining, whatever needed taking care of in Jenny's body. I imagine there was a lot, as very little kidney function had been occurring in that body for a long time. Also, she had an IV in her. As the IV bag emptied, the catheter bag would fill and fill and fill.

That night, I was restless. By nature, I am a light sleeper. Robin, on the other hand, sleeps like a rock. If there was an earthquake, Robin would not wake up. That first night, there was a machine next to my head that was going off constantly. It beeped incessantly and no one could figure out why. The dang buzzer kept waking me up. I then had to yell at Robin, who was sleeping through it, to shut that thing off. On top of that, Robin's cell was going off, which of course woke me up, but not her. So, in my weak and feeble state and with much difficulty, I had to confiscate Nurse Robin's cell.

Living in America - James Brown

On Independence Day, I woke up feeling nauseous. Every time I got out of bed to go to the bathroom, I was in a hurry to get back and lay still. Of course, I was hooked up to 90 things, so getting out of bed was a chore. The best thing was they had these tubes around my calves that inflated and moved my blood around a little bit. Those things were comfortable! Loved them. They were supposed to help prevent blood clots. I think I might need a pair for everyday living.

I also awoke to what would be a busy day filled with all kinds of visitors and goals. Yes, goals. Steve was nice enough to put them big and bright on the whiteboard for all visitors to see. He was also nice enough to put a check mark every time I accomplished something. The nurses loved it, although some thought he was adding undeserved checks.

1. Walk four times.

2. Sit in the chair three times.

3. Pass gas twice.

Listen, Do You Want to Know a Secret - The Beatles

The best thing about this entire experience was getting updates from Jenny's room. She was just down the hall, maybe four or five rooms away from us. Steve would go back and forth a lot. Getting updates on Jenny was such a huge boost. You know, you don't really know for sure if this transplant thing is going to work. Think about that for a second. I know I have been talking about this a lot. But it actually happened. It is happening now. An organ came out of my body and was inserted into someone else and began to work immediately. It's unbelievable. It's a miracle.

I admit, I was a little worried. Worried that maybe it wouldn't take. You just don't know for sure. So, Robin and I were hanging on every update from Steve. He would come in with these updates of unreal amounts of fluid filling up Jenny's drainage bag. Felix was working overtime, filtering massive amounts of fluids that had been building for who knows how long?

This morning, they woke Jenny up at 4:00 AM. Steve said it was pretty ugly, but they took her vitals, changed the bags and put her on the scale. She had lost seven pounds since getting a new kidney yesterday! Are you kidding me?! Seven pounds of water weight. I was curious, so I looked it up. One gallon of water weighs 8.6 lbs. She's closing in on a full gallon! Felix was eating it up and spitting it out.

Her kidney, which was my kidney, was in overdrive, pumping out all the fluid that the old kidney could not handle. Felix was an animal. He was going to town, taking care of business, and any other cliche you can think of. On one of my walks, we stopped to see Jenny. She had IV bags above her and the line went into her neck. And then you looked down and there was a bag catching all the urine. And it was moving continuously as her body was just flushing. Seeing her progress was really awesome. She even walked around with a walker. She stopped in to see us and it was super cool.

I felt crappy in the morning but better as the day went on. By 2:00, I wanted food. I was on a clear diet until now, so it was broth and Jello when I did eat. It was Wednesday afternoon and I had not eaten since Monday. At 4:45 PM, I acquired a sandwich, and I was the happiest kidney donor in the world!

The focus of the day, however, was not about food and regrettably, was not about our national independence either. The most uttered phrase by every nurse, nutritionist, supervisor, physician assistant, educator, and doctor who entered my room was, "I have never seen anything like that." The subject, of course, was my ginormous, protruding belly button.

Robin said she did not know whether to laugh or cry. I was doing both. It was funny! But what the heck was I going to do with this? It's going to go down, right? I will eventually have my innie restored to its proper place, right? I cannot live life with an outie!

There were a lot of people checking on me that day. Dr. Brightside, Nurse Teresa, Dr. Sew, all their assistants and personnel and the list goes on and on. I mean we were quite busy socializing. To all the medical personnel who came in, Robin would ask, "Is this normal?" As she gestured to my belly. To which they would reply, "No, that is not normal...I have never seen anything like that before."

You know I am all about firsts, but this was ridiculous. Eventually, people I didn't even know came in only to look at the whack-a-mole extending out of my belly. Women were talking about being hugely pregnant and even then, said their belly buttons did not stick out like this. Even a group of students came in to take a look and once again, I was the talk of the town.

Dr. Harvest's assistant or second in command took pictures and came back with an explanation of the phenomenon. You will recall that, during the surgery, Dr. Harvest was going to repair an umbilical hernia, which he did do. The assistant told us that Harvest was supposed to tack that belly button down from the inside after the repair. This was not done and therefore the once subtle innie was now reaching out and screaming for attention.

Pack It Up, Pack It In, Let Me Begin - House of Pain

Eventually, someone came in with a surgical kit. Some scissors and lots of gauze and tape. At first, I was thinking, oh, my gosh, they are going to pop it and drain this thing! But I came to my senses pretty quick as that would have killed me because my entire belly was swollen with fluid. She said, "we're just going to train the belly button to go back in...The fluid is going to be reabsorbed by the body, but the belly button needs to be trained to stay in. She pushed the button back into the belly, stuffed it with gauze and taped it up.

Problem solved! That is until the mole got lonely and burst the tape and gauze and came up for some air. We then went with cotton balls and extra tape.

Nurse Downer came to see me. I wondered if she thought I was mad at her. I was not of course. She is the one, you may recall, I was talking to the day before surgery when we were getting on the plane, and I was not cleared to donate. She cleared me later that day after Robin and I had lunch with the Petersens. I had never met her face to face. I was happy to see her and everyone. Getting to this point. I mean, this is a miracle that we are here. This actually happened.

Steve came in and said, "I want to introduce you to some people." Jenny's mom and dad walked in. I had never met them. Jenny's mom was crying and shaking before she came in the door and I could not understand what she was saying, but I knew it was the sincerest expression of thankfulness. Jenny's dad said, "I just don't know how to thank you." I was just...I did not know what to say either. It was all very emotional.

I had thought a lot about what the Petersens had gone through to get to this point, but I did not think much about their parents and extended family. I mean, I knew people were involved and invested, but now I had real faces to look at with real tears of emotion and appreciation for what we had done. More of Steve and Jenny's family and friends came in to introduce themselves and say thank you. Some, you could tell, were trying to hold back the tears. Some with success and others, not so much.

It was difficult yet rewarding meeting these people. I was grateful to be in a position where I could provide an organ and save a life. These strangers kept walking into my room with emotion on their faces and

190

trembling in their words. They shook my hands, and some embraced me, which isn't easy to do when you're mostly horizontal in a hospital bed with tubes and wires everywhere. It was so humbling. The Petersen kids came in for a brief visit and that was really fun. I simply kept saying things like, "It was my pleasure...we are just happy to be in a situation where we can help." I really meant it, but it seemed like an inadequate response.

Having my goals written on the whiteboard was a great ice breaker for these emotional visits. It was a good talking point. "So, I see you have met your goal today for passing gas. Good for you!" The belly button thing was also a major source of humor as the tape kept ripping off my belly and the beast would rear its ugly head.

After my belly button had been taped down and exploded and taped down and exploded a few times, we got the handle on things. Then the theme of the day switched to: "What do you get somebody who gave a kidney?" When all my new friends arrived, conversation eventually got around to the card or gift bag in their hand. They all thought, what do you give someone who gave a kidney? It's not every day you are in that position. I'm giving the gift givers an A+.

I am not a big gift giver or taker. I give gifts, but my wife is way better at it, so that is her department. I'm not huge on receiving either. Had I had the chance, I would have told all the givers to save their energy and money and please forgo the ritual. But laying there in that bed, it did feel good to have some chocolate or know Robin and I would be eating out together soon. These cards and goodie bags came from people we do not even know. Lots of snacks, gift cards for movie streaming services and food, were much appreciated, and would be put to good use immediately.

All non-staff visitors were from the Petersens' family and friends. I do have family and friends in the area, but I did not tell anyone. Only my immediate family and church friends at home knew I was going under the knife. No social media, no casual mentions to friends. It just did not feel right. I did get two visitors, however, Dan and Karen Adams—Dan is my dad's first cousin. Well, they came wandering in and needless to say, I was really surprised. I'm guessing my dad made a call. Super cool of them to drop in!

I ate well beginning with the 4:00 PM sandwich. Everything was on the menu from the hospital plus the junk food being smuggled in. I had a good sandwich, chips, salad, and a lemon meringue pie for dinner. As the day wound down, visitors stopped coming and the goals on the board read:

1. Walk four times. //// Nailed it!

2. Sit in the chair three times. /// Rocked it!

3. Pass gas twice. //// Crushed it!

Following a good dinner, we turned our sofa around, so it faced out the window where we had a partial view of the Salt Lake Valley. The best part about our room, however, was our location to the helipad which we were almost directly facing. We had fireworks but did not get the grand fireworks show we were hoping for. However, we did have a front row seat for three helicopters coming and going. At one point, 15 people were on the helipad helping patients exit.

It was nice. Robin and I sat there with our feet up on the window just watching the goings on of the outside world. It was quiet except for a little Fourth of July music we were playing. Steve gave me some Fourth of July socks, which I was wearing for the occasion. It was a really cool and peaceful evening staring out that window. We eventually turned in. I made sure the beeping machine was fixed and Robin's ringer was on SILENT, and I slept like a baby.

July 5, 2018

Take Me Home - John Denver

I was up before the sun this morning, which in July in Utah is before 6:00 AM. I am excited to leave this place. Don't get me wrong, we have had an amazing stay. Best kidney donation ever! Great service, great company, good food, splendid room and accommodations, but I'm ready to free up my bed for the next giver.

The morning was filled with the usual questions. "How's your pain?" "How's your belly button?" "Have you pooped yet?" Fine, fine, and nope. I had a fantastic poop on Tuesday morning, thanks to the delicious lunch at the Red Iguana the day before. But now we are on Thursday. So, we need to think about making that happen.

My goals for the day were again written on the board. I won't bore you with that again, but yes, having a bowel movement was on the list. Today, I will walk a little further, my gut will get a little better, and I will progress.

My walks were more like a walk around the neighborhood, where you stop and talk to your neighbors. We stopped in to see the Petersens. Jenny was well, Steve was fine, and Felix was still killing it. They would not be going home today. Perhaps tomorrow for them. As we continued, we ran into many of the staff who had been visiting my room. I told them all I was leaving today and, as you can imagine, they were all so sad to see me go (sarcasm).

We ran into Dr. Harvest, who I did not see yesterday, only his assistant came by. He apologized for my new outie belly button. He said it was an easy procedure that he had missed where you simply tack down the belly button following the hernia repair. He told me he would make it right. I said, let's wait to see what happens. At that moment, going back under the knife to fix anything was not an appealing thought.

Harvest was cool and it was good to talk to him. I had questions about the procedure because I find it really interesting. As we spoke, I could not help but think that this man put his hand through my belly and pulled out a kidney. And I'm standing here less than 48 hours later talking to him about it. He told me I was made to donate. My kidney, my body, everything was tailor made to donate a kidney. He even said how well it was performing in Jenny. I told him that the kidney had a new name, Felix. So, you can call him Felix. It's just easier.

Later that afternoon, they wheeled me down the stairs and out the door. I transferred to a car, where Nurse Robin was now Chauffeur Robin, and we drove south to Draper, Utah and checked into Spyglass Rehab

194

and Wellness Center (AKA my Aunt Connie and Uncle Rob's house).

Part 3
RECOVERY

July 5-7, 2018

All I Have to Do is Dream, Dream Dream Dream... - The Everly Brothers

The transplant team told me that I was not allowed to go home until they had cleared me. They said, plan on a two-week stay at my aunt and uncle's. My first morning, I woke up early feeling really good. Robin and I took a walk around the neighborhood and sat on a park bench for a while. When we got back to the house, I was energized, and we decided to go see a movie.

We needed to leave in 20 minutes, so I told Robin I was just going to lay down for a minute. But when my face hit the pillow, there was no stopping it. Four and a half hours later, I woke in a fog, wondering where I was. I was really groggy and, with all my strength, called Nurse Robin. She explained that, when it was time to leave for the movie, I was heavy in dreamland and could not be disturbed.

And so it was for the rest of the week. Lots of sleeping and down time. I took walks every day and went a little farther each time. I attended the temple, which was right down the street, and I felt a little better every day.

July 8, 2018

Birthday - The Beatles

Today was Sunday, the day of rest. And yet, I knew it would be the least restful day for me. I wasn't sure how I was going to pull this day off. When I pulled the trigger on the July 3rd donation date, there were several events that did not jibe with that decision. But what are you gonna do? Had to make the call. One of those events was Robin's birthday, which is tomorrow. However, Robin flies home tomorrow morning and I needed to do something for her today.

I did not know how I would feel five days post operation, but I decided to be optimistic and throw her a surprise birthday party today. Our families are from Utah, so we have family and friends who live in the area. Thanks to Uncle Rob, who reserved the neighborhood clubhouse and my sister-in-law, Nikki, who provided cake and ice cream, the event was a total success.

The Petersens, minus Jenny, showed up, as did cousins, aunts, uncles, and friends. It was really a cool evening.

July 9, 2018

Roll With the Changes - REO Speedwagon

My sweetheart flew home this morning on her birthday. What a great experience this was to have with my wife. And I mean, from beginning to end. The decision to donate, all the testing, the passes and failures, EVERYTHING. She was my partner through all of it. Because she is a nurse, she is much more adept at making medical decisions than I am. I leaned on her continually for information and decisions.

Although it was my body that gifted a kidney, it was every bit as much from Robin as from me. This whole thing would have never happened without her. It was tough letting her go this morning, but we had kids at home and lives to resume. Jenny's sister and sister-in-law, who tag teamed our kids this last week did an amazing job and now they were done.

Should I Stay or Should I Go - The Clash

Originally, I thought I would stay in a hotel for my recovery time. You know, not bug or be a burden on anyone. Just get a hotel and chill for 10 days until they let me go. But I could not have made a better choice than staying with Uncle Rob and Aunt Connie. They are as cool as they come and are great company. Plus, if I needed anything, they were on it. They had all these great trails by their house, which I pretty much ruled by the end of my stay.

My son Eli is my best buddy. I miss that kid like crazy, but as a five-year-old with Down Syndrome, had he been around for my recovery, I would be back in the hospital with some injury. We roll around and play all the time. Hugs are abundant. He crawls in my bed every night and kicks like crazy. Not the best for a speedy recovery.

July 10-16, 2018

Carry On Wayward Son - Kansas

Week two of recovery was much like week one. Lots of rest followed by more and more walking. The trails above Draper, Utah became my training grounds and refuge. Every day, I would retreat to those trails and go for miles. I really loved it, as it not only got me going physically but cleared my head and soul. Uncle Rob walked with me at times, and I even got a cousin to join me once.

I had a lot of swelling in my gut area, which diminished a little more every day. I put my laptop to use, and got stuff done on the work front. The University of Utah Medical Center had me checking my blood pressure every morning and evening and I was looking good. I had a physical at the University and they told me I was fit to go home. And so, exactly two weeks after flying into Salt Lake City, I returned home.

July 17-31, 2018

Catch A Wave - The Beach Boys

Upon my return to San Diego, the summer was in full swing, and I could not wait to get back in the water. Surf temp was 75 degrees, which is really warm for San Diego, and I jumped in way before the doc told me it was safe to do so. Okay, I didn't jump. I eased in. I couldn't help it, plus the ocean has always been the best healer for me.

I kept in touch with Steve and Jenny. Felix had morphed into a lovable animated character by now. The kids in both families had drawn cartoons of the kidney. There were kidney pillows, stained glass, stickers, and more. The Petersens reported that Felix was hard at work with massive filtration, which was making Jenny healthier by the day.

We continued to joke about Felix's appetite and stamina Each week, we hit a new mark and received solid updates. Updates from me were that I continued to push myself and occasionally would get slapped down. Naps were not uncommon. Jenny reported, "I never expected to be feeling this good this quickly."

Getting updates like that were exciting, as we were both ahead of schedule and headed in the right direction. Kids and family became more demanding, and life got back to normal.

Movin' Right Along - Alkaline Trio

Weekly health updates turned into monthly, and then quarterly. A couple of years went by, and Steve got a job in L.A. And just like that, the Petersens were two hours north of us. We see each other at least twice a year, which includes a mandatory dinner every year around the donation anniversary. We recall the journey, the failures, successes, and shake our heads that we pulled it off. It seems like every time we go down memory lane, we learn something new. Four years post-surgery, I found out that Felix is living in Jenny's front abdomen area, not the back! Apparently, this is where transplanted kidneys are generally placed, not where they came from in the back. Jenny can actually feel Felix! How cool is that!?

Part 4

Final Thoughts

Remember the message Teresa left on my phone, when I failed the iothalamate test? I still have it. It reminds me of the instances on this journey when doctors and science told me I should quit when I knew in my gut I should keep fighting. Fortunately for me and Jenny and the many other people affected by my actions, my gut was right.

Transplant Games of America

My family and I celebrated my fifth-year donation anniversary by attending and participating in the Transplant Games of America. It happened to be in my hometown, so how could I not go? The games are mostly catered to organ recipients but have plenty of events for donors. If you ever get the chance to go, please do; it's like a mini-Olympics with all kinds of events.

Even if you have no connection to the transplant world, this is a bucket list event. Imagine attending an event with thousands of people who should not be alive. It's inspiring, to say the least.

I met a man who was in the hospital in Los Angeles with a rapidly declining heart. He had accepted his fate with death and was preparing to die, when, suddenly, his doctor told him a heart was on the way. Someone had died in Seattle and a heart was being flown to a recipient in Miami. The recipient in Miami had passed away while the heart was en route. The plane then banked hard right and diverted to Los

Angeles, where this other man got a new lease on life.

I met a family who lost their teenage daughter a week prior to the games. Her organs and tissue went to save and improve the lives of others. They heard the games were in town and they came to mingle and take them in. Mother, father, and siblings, still grieving over the tragic loss of this beautiful, young member of the family—they came and were embraced.

I met a man who should have died in a car accident. His entire body was severely burned. Most of the skin on his body, including his entire head, was replaced with someone else's skin.

The list goes on and on. Heart, kidney, liver, eyes, lungs, skin, and so forth. Several people are receiving transplants over and over again. I'm telling you, it's like nothing I have ever experienced. Ever hang out with someone who has been granted a new lease on life? It tends to change people. Imagine walking into a convention hall where thousands of people who should be dead are competing against and embracing one another.

You cannot imagine how much life you feel, when you are mingling with those who should be dead.

It was during these games that I decided to publish my journal. Specifically, my decision came at the most somber moment of the games. They were playing a slide show of all the Transplant Games participants from past years who have since died. What a powerful moment that was to experience.

I stopped looking at the screen and turned to see the reactions on people's faces. Tears, love, and compassion were emulating from the audience as they recognized their fellow recipients who were only there in spirit this year.

Seventeen people in the United States die every day while waiting for a transplant. Unfortunately, death is something this community is all too familiar with. But it doesn't have to be that way.

To Those of You Who Need an Organ, Eye, or Tissue

Last I checked, there are over 120,000 of you. I cannot imagine what it is like to be in your shoes. What a helpless and humbling experience to be completely reliant on someone else. I have met many of you. Some who have simply lost hope, given up, and passed away.

Please do not give up! I have rubbed shoulders with hundreds of people who received life-saving gifts and their stories are inspiring. If your needs can be met with a living donation, know there are an infinite number of good people out there willing to help. PLEASE ASK. I know you might not want to but do! Be creative and proactive. People will help you.

To Those of You Who Might Consider Being a Live Donor

This is a BIG deal. Don't go into it lightly, but please consider it.

- If one in every 10,000 people in the U.S. who are eligible to donate a kidney chose to donate, the waiting list would be gone.
- Ninety percent of live kidney donors say they would do it again. I am among that 90%

There is a small sign on my desk that reads, "I am chasing moments." I love moments big, small, and everything in between. They make a person who he or she is. They mold and define you. Our lives are made up of moments. I choose to chase moments that will make me and my family better.

Donating a kidney was a supreme moment in my life. What I learned about myself and the effect it had on me cannot be found any other way. I have always felt that selfless acts of service determine one's happiness. People who give and serve are the happiest and most successful people on earth. Would you agree? If so, why? I believe it's because giving creates extraordinary moments.

How often do you get to save a life or give someone something to sustain life and quality of life? How often do you get to be an answer to someone's prayers? I don't know if I could ever find a more rewarding moment.

Jenny's uncle, Tom Clyde, writes for the Park Record, a local publication in Park City. He wrote the following about organ donation. He's talking about me and Jenny.

Registering As an Organ Donor is a Small Task to Make a Big Difference
by Tom Clyde

I'm looking at a photo my sister sent me. It's of her daughter – my niece – and a man none of us know. They are both in hospital gowns, smiling, and looking inexplicably relaxed given what is about to happen. Anybody looking at the picture would think they are a good-looking young couple. You'd never assume they were strangers. What's really happening is that they are both about to go into surgery where he will donate a kidney to my niece.

Nice to meet you.

There are really no protocols for that relationship. Facebook has no button to click to describe your relationship as "Live Organ Donation." The donor is a stranger. He's a friend of a friend's cousin's neighbor or something like that. He heard about my niece's kidney failure somehow, and decided he would give her a kidney. Why not? The only bond is that they are both parents of children with Down syndrome. The man considered the challenges their children face, and how much harder their lives would be if they were without a parent. So, after months of testing, he and his wife flew up from California and gave her a kidney.

The two couples went to dinner the night before the surgeries. It's hard to imagine that conversation. The whole thing is so surreal. They probably talked about their handicapped kids and the challenges their whole families face there. Maybe a little World Cup action, while steering clear of politics, and, oh, by the way, thank you for putting your life at risk to save mine. It's really nice to meet you. We'll pick up the check for dinner. Amazing.

The donor is a stranger. … He heard about my niece's kidney failure somehow, and decided he would give her a kidney. Why not?"

You just don't pick up a kidney at Home Depot. Within a large and supportive family, she had been unable to find a suitable match. Most of us were categorically disqualified because of age, blood pressure, and other issues. The screening system knocked me out almost before I got my name entered. Apparently, high blood pressure puts me at risk of someday needing to find a replacement kidney, and they aren't about to let me give one up. Her sister was generally compatible, but kidneys aren't as standardized as you'd think, and the plumbing didn't match up.

There are complicated trades, where a donor who is incompatible with his or her family member donates to a stranger who matches, and somebody in that stranger's circle of potential donors turns out to be compatible with your family member. The hospitals almost run a brokerage on them.

I'll confess to being somewhat relieved that I wasn't an acceptable match. I was so summarily rejected that I never really had to come face to face with the decision. I think I would have made the donation for my niece, but it's easy to say that when you're punted out of the system on the first question. Would I donate a kidney to a total stranger? Well, um, boy, it's been a long time since we had any rain around here.

When nobody in the extended family is a suitable match, you begin casting the net a little wider. She didn't exactly start calling best friends from second grade and asking for a kidney but did put the word out there. She had an overwhelming response among friends, but nothing matched. It's not an easy request. "Would you take care of my dog next weekend?" is one thing, but to add, "and by the way, I need a kidney," is quite another. And a year passed, and then a couple more, and nothing happened until a random stranger came along and made an incredible sacrifice.

The surgery seems both miraculous and routine. Pull one from the parts bin, take the old one out; sew the new one in. Within just minutes, the donated organ was functioning properly. She was on the mend almost immediately. The donor may have a more difficult recovery. In addition to major surgery, his remaining kidney needs to pick up the full load. Nobody is leaving the hospital for a while. The medical team involved made it all seem routine. They knock out several of these a week.

My father knew Willem Kolff, who was the inventor of dialysis. I remember him being at our house when I was young, talking about the mechanical, artificial kidney, and saying miraculous as it was, the future was organ transplant, not his machines. Maybe in the not-too-distant future, we will be making new organs on 3D printers from our own cells.

For the time being, the option is organ transplant. It's easy to become an organ donor, and if you do it after you are dead, it's also not frightening or an act of great courage. You won't be needing your organs when you're gone. Go to YesUtah.org and register online. It's that easy.

To Everyone

Please sign up to be an organ donor via your state's registry. I am quite sure you will have no use for anything on your body when you are dead. Why not save a life?

- One organ donor can save the lives of up to eight people.
- One tissue donor can help enhance the lives of 75 people.

How Will I Know - Whitney Houston

At the time of this publishing, we are just shy of celebrating our six-year donation anniversary. Six years of single kidney. I would like to answer the most important question for a kidney donor. It's the one I asked myself before and after donating, and the one I get asked most often. That is, "how has the donation affected you?"

Overwhelmingly, both from myself and from my polling fellow donors, this answer is a resounding, "ALL GOOD." Personally, the only time I ever notice I am down a kidney is when somebody brings it up. I don't miss Felix. Although please don't tell him. Or is it her? I have never not participated in a physical activity because I was down a kidney.

There are moments when I drag at the end of the day or feel a little funny. And there are moments when I ask myself if I feel off because I'm getting older, fatter, or is it possibly kidney-related? The mind is powerful and that thought does creep in, though it is rare, and I usually dismiss it. Physically, my life has not changed. I am as active as I have time to be, and I have not noticed any difference in my physical health. That is, with the exception of three occurrences.

1. One month after my donation, I was at Torrey Pines State Beach doing my favorite run. I felt weird and decided to push through it. When I got back to my car, I continued to decline. I went home, showered, and two hours later, I told my son to get the car and take me to Urgent Care. I vomited in the bushes and collapsed on the walkway.

   After an hour in urgent care, they put me in an ambulance and took me to the Emergency Room. No one, including Nurse Robin, could figure out what was wrong with me. I was freezing cold. They smothered me in hot blankets fresh out of the warmer, and I could not get warm. My body sucked down a few IV bags and I finally went home just before sun-up.

   Two days previous to this, I had attended the surprise birthday party of a friend. I found out later that this party was a "super spreader" event with several families hugging the throne. I have caught several stomach bugs in my life. What I am saying is that this time, my body reacted far more violently and differently than ever before. I believe that, had I not donated, it would have been far less dramatic.

2. One year after donation, I caught the flu and had a similar reaction. It was not a stomach flu, but my body had a similar, over-the-top reaction. I was starting to think that my body was going to handle illnesses differently without a second kidney. Or perhaps I just needed more time to adjust.

3. Two years post-surgery, our family went on a reality TV show called Survivalist. As part of the show, we competed against another family in challenges and a three-day adventure race. On day one of the adventure race, I felt great from beginning to end. I even slept okay despite my son's bloody nose in the middle of the night and the usual camping disruptions. By the end of day two, I started to feel sick. I felt nauseous, fatigued, and weird. I say weird, because it was a foreign feeling that I have never felt except for those two times I had gotten sick since my donation.

The competition was tight with the other family, which forced us to run through the mountains and not just hike. I did not think the weather, altitude, and exertion was enough to get to me. I was pounding the liquids and thought I was fine, except towards the end of day two when my body was letting me know that it was not well. I powered through the last segment of the day and looked forward to a restful night. I choked down some dinner and figured my body would rejuvenate that night. As the night progressed, my condition worsened. I did not sleep, but just lay there all night in my sleeping bag.

By morning, I was in bad shape. Our family had been battling together all week in a highly contested race, and on the morning of the final day, I was really sick. We were hiding from the other family because we did not want them to know I was sick. The producer told us we would have an hour penalty if I dropped out, which would ensure defeat. The medic team was all over me and, at one point, pulled me from the race until Robin convinced them otherwise.

We gathered as a family in prayer to ask our maker for help. What happened next was nothing short of a miracle and an answer to our prayers. I was walking alone and without a pack and I could literally feel myself getting stronger with every step. It was not long before I had a spring in my step and was pulling my daughter along, carrying a pack. I would say half-way through the day, I was at full strength and running as hard as anyone at the finish.

You can view the entire episode at: https://www.byutv.org/search?player-open=true&content-id=5a4df9e9-bf00-49ba-811f-c1dfe37acb04

Resources

American Association of Kidney Patients (AAKP):
https://aakp.org/
AAKP is a patient-led organization that provides resources and support for individuals with kidney

disease, including those considering or undergoing transplantation.

National Kidney Foundation: https://www.kidney.org
The National Kidney Foundation is dedicated to the awareness, prevention, and treatment of kidney disease. They help those who suffer from or are at risk of kidney disease.

National Kidney Registry:
https://www.kidneyregistry.org/
The National Kidney Registry is committed to increasing the number of kidney transplants from living donors, improving donor-recipient matching, and offering support to living kidney donors.

National Living Donor Assistance Center:
https://www.livingdonorassistance.org/
NLDAC provides financial assistance to living donors. They can help with travel and related expenses to individuals not otherwise eligible to afford these expenses.

United Network for Organ Sharing (UNOS):
https://unos.org/
UNOS is the nonprofit organization that coordinates U.S. organ transplant activities. UNOS also provides resources to help patients learn more about living donation.

Acknowledgements

To my family, friends, and the medical professionals who supported me during this transformative experience: Thank you. You made my journey possible.

To Jenny and Steve Petersen: You accepted a gift that helped me to understand selfless service. I could never have imagined how I would grow as a person because of it. Thank you.

To Teresa Nordquist: Thank you for being my advocate, for fighting for me, and for getting me through this entire process. I literally could not have done it without your help.

To the University of Utah Medical Center: You guys are top-notch. Thank you for providing me with a killer donation experience.

To my rad wife and the awesome Nurse Robin: Thank you for your unwavering love, for forever being by my side, and for walking, running, and skipping through life with me.

To my editor, Jen Gadbow: You managed to clean up my manuscript and keep my own words and voice in there. Thank you.

Finally, to the readers of this book, thank you for joining me on my journey as a kidney donor. It is my hope that this journal contributes to the broader conversation surrounding organ donation and encourages others to consider, not only the profound impact they can make through this selfless act, but also to imagine the intense, reflective, and life-changing experience of being an organ donor.

Made in the USA
Monee, IL
23 January 2024

51717249R00125